Pennywise Boutique

BARBARA L. FARLIE

Illustrations by Jean Simpson

CREATIVE HOME LIBRARY®
In Association with Better Homes and Gardens®
Meredith Corporation

⌂ CREATIVE HOME LIBRARY®

© 1974 by Meredith Corporation, Des Moines, Iowa

Library of Congress Cataloging in Publication Data

Farlie, Barbara L.
  Pennywise boutique.

  1. Dressmaking. 2. Dress accessories. 3. Handi-
craft. I. Title.
TT515.F28   646.4   73–15552
ISBN 0–696–36000–4

About the Author:

Barbara L. Farlie, who is also the author of another of the popular Creative Home Library craft books, *Beading: Basic and Boutique,* has had a lifelong interest in crafts and their creative applications. This interest has recently led her into the field of television, where she has served as co-hostess on the nationally syndicated program, "All About Crafts!" and made frequent guest appearances on other programs. She has also spoken on crafts before women's groups, has served as adviser on antiques to the UCLA Arts Council, and has taught a variety of crafts at the Adult School of Montclair, New Jersey.

Presently, Mrs. Farlie is craft consultant to the dean of students' office at Fairleigh Dickinson University in Rutherford, New Jersey. In addition, she is now at work on a book about antique types of dollhouses. Her personal interests and areas of expertise range from crafts to antiques, from fashion design to interior decoration and architecture. She makes her home with her husband, their three children, and a collie, in Upper Montclair, New Jersey.

Contents

Pennywise Boutique

Preface

If you have ever yearned for a custom-made gown featured on a television commercial, suffered pangs of envy at the sight of a movie star's bejeweled evening collar, dreamed about owning the fantastic beaded necklace offered at a fantastic beaded price at an "in" boutique—then *this* is the book for you! I have written *Pennywise Boutique* to show you how to create your own glamorous fashions and accessories instantly and inexpensively, by using craft methods and techniques that formerly had no place in fashion and sewing.

Because I am not a professional seamstress, I have devised all sorts of shortcuts and used time-saving craft techniques in order to dress as elegantly as my talented sewing sisters. If I can do it, you can, too! Even those of you who don't sew a stitch (either because you've never tried or because you have tried and failed) can now go creative and, with minimal expense and effort on your part, make elegant and useful clothing, accessories, and gifts for yourself, your family, and your friends.

Many of these projects require no sewing at all. Those that do may be done either by hand or by machine, if you have one. Even today my only sewing machine is a hand-me-down portable. My mother, who was a Depression-era bride, presented it to me when I married. Despite my protests that I'd have no use for it, she insisted that I take the machine if only, as she put it, "to mend sheets." A sheet I've never mended, a sewing course I've never taken, but that trusty portable has seen me through maternity and baby garments, playclothes and evening wear. Most recently I've used it to make the smocks that Vivian Abell and I wear on our syndicated television show, "All About Crafts!" My old machine does not do one fancy stitch; it has no attachments and sews only in forward and reverse. But for my method of sewing, it works like a charm. I'm basically a lazy sewer and prefer spending my free time with my family rather than closeted away making clothes. Although I've written this book to pass on my "trade secrets" to other lazy sewers like myself, I think that even a proficient sewer will gain great satisfaction in expanding her repertoire of skills with these craft techniques, which might never have occurred to her and which can at the very least save many precious minutes.

My slightly unorthodox approach is to tackle the art of sewing strictly in craft terms—the only terms with which I am completely familiar. I justify myself by pointing out that this approach is in keeping with the life we live today. Just as we're all in favor of jiffy cooking at times, so it stands to reason that at times we may want to eliminate time-consuming steps associated with traditional sewing by taking advantage of craft techniques and shortcuts. That does not mean to deny the value of the gourmet cook's perfect soufflé or the talented seamstress's French-tailored gown. But when time is of the essence, it shouldn't be spent on time-consuming details.

Pennywise Boutique is a collection, or a potpourri, of craft fashion projects that are easy to make, elegant to look at, and fun to wear. Best of all, nothing in the book costs more than $20 to make or takes more than a few hours to complete. In fact, many of the projects cost less than a dollar or two and can be completed in a matter of minutes.

The multitude of ideas in *Pennywise Boutique* should give everyone, in this era of mass production, many suggestions for achieving personal satisfaction in handcrafting. Perhaps it's just a token of revolt against the mechanization of the world today when, instead of running out to buy something ready-made for a gift or a special occasion, we take the time and effort to make the item ourselves.

I have tried to provide a kaleidoscope of craft fashion projects that will dazzle and delight you. It is my fond wish that this book will trigger your imagination and that you will find, within your fingertips, the power to create a new and personal fashion concept for a look that's ''you.''

I am especially grateful to my sister Judith L. Hauser for her invaluable advice and help on many of the projects in the book. Without Judy, this book might never have become a reality. I am also grateful to my husband, William N. Farlie, Jr., for patiently reading and rereading the manuscript and offering suggestions; to my children Lisa, Billy, and Craig for their help on the children's and boys' projects; to my parents, Blanche and Herman Leitzow, for their advice on the manuscript; to my other sister, Nancy L. Brown, for project ideas; and last, but certainly not least, to Vivian M. Abell, my dear friend, for her invaluable project contributions.

1
Never
Sew
Unless
You
Want
to

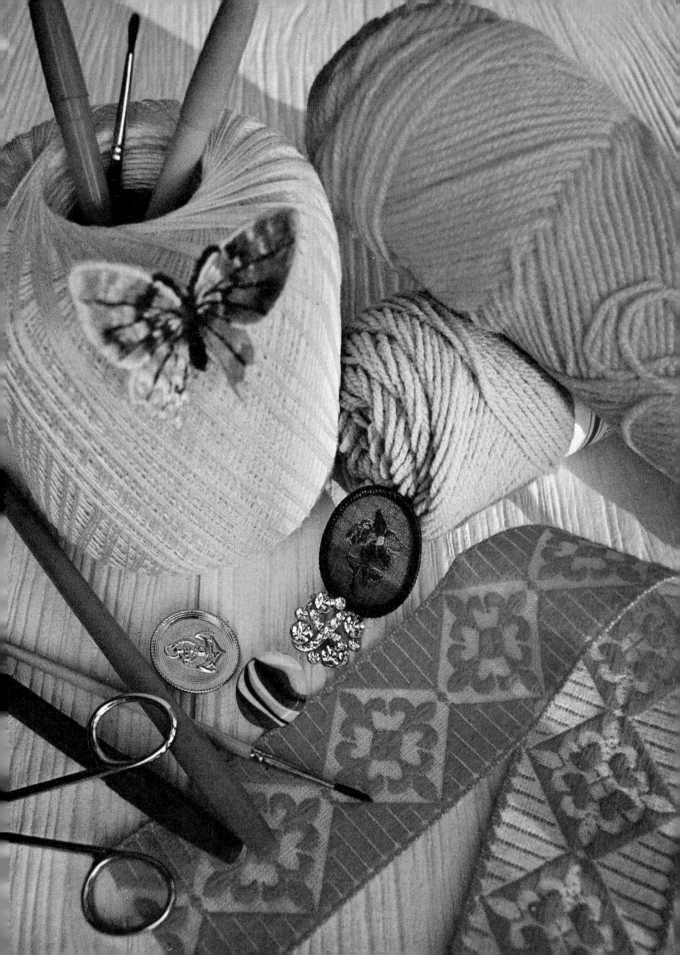

The main credo of this book, and its continuing theme, is: Never sew unless you want to! Learn to use a craft approach, instead. Whenever it comes to a choice between sewing and gluing, I glue. One mother of six girls that I know hasn't put up a hem by conventional methods in years. She uses white resin craft glue to do the hems instead. Because the white resin glue is dry-cleanable but not washable, she takes the girls' dresses and school uniforms to the local self-service dry cleaner. When she is ready to change the hemline, a short soak in cool water releases the bond; after the garment dries it can be reglued at the new hemline.

However, a minimum knowledge of basic techniques and equipment is necessary for the craft approach. Much of it you probably know or, in the case of materials, already have on hand. But if you don't, it won't take you weeks to learn or cost you an arm and a leg to procure the equipment.

So, since your technique is vital to the success of these projects, it's worth taking time to read this chapter thoroughly. Those who are already proficient in certain skills, such as macramé, may want to skip over the beginners' directions for these crafts. Be sure, however, to read the sections on crafts and techniques that you are not familiar with.

Basic Supplies

The following is an alphabetical list of supplies needed for the projects in this book. If you are making only a few projects, you will need only the supplies called for under ''materials'' in each project. (The list does not include the obvious supplies you are certain to have on hand, such as a pencil, chalk, a ruler, straight pins, a pressing or thin cotton cloth, an iron, an ironing board, a pair of scissors, a sewing machine or needle and thread, and a pair of pliers or tweezers.)

This supply list may seem lengthy, but only a fraction of the items are necessary for any one project, and most are very inexpensive. All in all, you can easily get started with enough equipment to make most of the projects for less than $10.

Acrylic paint: Permanent, easy to use, water soluble, and quick drying, for craft projects and textiles. Made in a wide range of colors, in jar or tube. Sold at craft, hobby, dime, and hardware stores.

Artist's paintbrushes: Small brushes for applying liquids—glue, paint, finishes, and the like—made of sable, nylon, or bristle, in ⅛-inch diameter or larger; best brush for most projects is ¼- to ½-inch nylon brush sold at craft, hobby, dime, art supply, and hardware stores.

Ball fringe: Cotton decorative fringe with tiny balls. Made in a wide range of colors and color combinations, with ½- or 1-inch diameter balls. Sold by the yard or fraction thereof, at fabric and notions stores and departments.

Beads: Small round objects with a hole for stringing or sewing, made of wood, glass, plastic, metal, in all sizes, shapes, and colors. Available on strings or singly in the case of larger beads. Sold at fabric, craft, and notions stores and departments.

Beaded trim: Lavish bead designs stitched to thin cotton or net backing. Made in a wide range of colors, styles, and widths. Sold by the yard, at fabric and notions stores and departments.

Bonding net: Fusible, weblike material sold under brand names such as Stitch Witchery and Poly Web. Used with an iron to bond two pieces of fabric together. Available in packages in the form of narrow strips and by the yard, 18 inches wide. Sold at fabric and notions stores and departments.

Brads: Brass fasteners for paper. Sold at stationery and dime stores.

Braid: Braided or woven trimming, in a wide range of colors, designs, and widths. Sold by the yard, at fabric and notions stores.

Button snaps: A combination button and snap that permits garment closure with the look of a button but without a buttonhole. The button part is a metal base, which is intended to be covered with fabric. Made in a single, domelike shape, in several different sizes. Sold six to eight to a package, at fabric and notions stores and departments.

Canvas mesh: Open-weave canvas for needlepoint. Made in white or tan colors, in various size meshes expressed in terms of the number of meshes to the inch. Sold in pieces or by the yard, at needlework and craft stores and departments.

Commercial patterns: Printed sewing patterns for making clothes, home decor, and craft items. Made in a wide variety of styles and sizes, as illustrated in pattern books. Sold at fabric, dime, and department stores.

Cording (see also *Upholstery cording):* Tubular trim over a cotton cord base; used for edgings. Made in a wide range of colors and in several different sizes. Sold prepackaged in short lengths or by the yard, at fabric and notions stores and departments.

Crochet-look fabric: Open-weave acrylic fabric, which simulates hand-crochet work in appearance. Made in a wide array of colors and patterns. Sold by the yard, 45 inches wide, at fabric stores and departments.

Cupboard hinges: Metal hardware used on cupboard doors to enable them to open. For these projects, decorative hinges made of brass or other ornamental metals are best, in sizes no larger than 2 by 2½ inches. Sold at hardware stores and some craft shops.

Curtain rings: Rings for suspending curtains or draperies from rods. Made in a wide array of sizes, shapes, materials, and colors. Sold several to a package, at fabric, upholstery, and dime stores.

Decorative yarn gift tie: Loosely twisted, puffy yarn for tying gift packages or children's hair. Made in a wide range of colors. Sold in short lengths or on a card or spool, at dime stores and card stores.

Door chain lock: Sliding chain closure for locking doors. Made in brass, brass plate, or nickel, in several sizes and weights. Sold at hardware stores.

Elastic: Stretchy rubber for waistbands, cuffs, etc. Made in white and black, in a wide range of widths. Sold in short lengths on cards, or by the yard, at fabric and notions stores and departments.

Elastic thread: Stretchy thread for sewing. Made in white and black only. Sold on a spool, at fabric and notions stores and departments.

Embroidery floss: Shiny cotton thread, usually of six strands, for embroidery. Made in a wide range of colors and multicolor combinations. Sold in small skeins, at needlework, fabric, and dime stores.

Embroidered trim: Cotton, velvet, rayon, or satin ribbon, elaborately embroidered, sometimes with metallic thread. Made in a wide range of designs, colors, and widths. Sold at fabric and notions stores and departments.

Eyelet edging: Decorative cotton or nylon edging with punched-out holes. Made in several colors, in many different widths and styles. Sold packaged in small lengths or by the yard, at fabric and notions stores and departments.

Fake fur: Synthetic fabric that resembles fur. Made in a wide range of colors, styles, and thicknesses. Sold in wide widths, 60 inches and wider, at fabric stores and departments.

Felt: Fabric of pressed 100-percent wool or, more commonly, a combination of wool and rayon. Made in a variety of vibrant colors. Sold by the yard, in 72-inch widths, at fabric stores and departments, or in precut rectangles, 9 by 12 inches or 12 by 15 inches, at dime, fabric, and craft stores.

Felt-tipped markers: Soft-pointed pens with thick or thin points, for decorative lettering or drawing. Made in a wide range of colors, water soluble or waterproof. Sold at craft, dime, art, and stationery stores.

Foam rubber: Rubber for filling pillows, padding, etc. Made in white only, in several thicknesses. Sold precut in various sizes, by the yard, or shredded in bags, at fabric and notions stores and departments.

Fold-over braid: Cotton, rayon, or acrylic trim, folded lengthwise, used to finish the raw edge of a garment. Made in a wide range of colors. Designed to be sandwiched over edge of fabric; top edge is slightly narrower to allow catching of underneath edge when stitched. Made in one style and two widths, ½ inch and 1 inch (folded width). Sold at fabric and notions stores and departments.

Fringe: Decorative cotton, acrylic, rayon, or silk trim, in a wide range of colors; several different styles, sizes, thicknesses. Sold on a card or singly, at fabric and notions stores and departments.

Gimp upholstery braid: Decorative edging for

18

upholstery to conceal nails; also used in crafts. Made in a wide range of colors, but in only one style, ½ inch wide. Sold by the yard, at fabric, notions, and upholstery stores and departments.

Glitter Magic: Brand name; glitter and glue in a single tube to decorate fabrics or paper; manufactured by Walco-Linck Corporation. Sold in small tubes, in several colors, at craft and dime stores.

Glow Writer: Brand name for plastic tool that writes in vibrant colors; manufactured by Walco-Linck Corporation. Sold in a tube, at craft and dime stores.

Glue: Liquid or paste bonding material for projects in this book. Best is Sobo, manufactured by Sloman's Laboratories, a white resin, water-soluble glue, which dries colorless, is nonflammable, and bonds well. Sobo is sold at craft, dime, hardware, and fabric stores.

Gold cord gift tie: Metallic cord for wrapping gift packages; also used in crafts. Available in silver also. Sold on a spool or roll, at upholstery, fabric, and notions stores and departments.

Hemp braid: Woven trim made of hemp. Available in natural color only, in different widths. Sold at upholstery, fabric, and notions stores and departments.

Jewelry findings: Backs for pins, earrings, and cuff links and clasps for necklaces. Made in various sizes, styles, and metals. Sold at craft stores, or check the Yellow Pages for nearest supplier.

Knitting yarn: Usually of wool or acrylic, in a wide range of colors. Available in different plies or thicknesses, in skeins of various weights or on cards in the case of mending yarn. Sold at yarn, needlework, and notions stores and departments.

Macramé board or pillow: Styrofoam rectangle, foam rubber pillow, or gypsum board, about 12 by 15 inches, for holding pinned macramé work while it is in process. Sold at craft and dime stores.

Masking tape: Opaque, protective, adhesive-backed tape. Made in tan only, in several different widths. Sold at paint and hardware stores and departments.

Metallic ribbon and trim: Ribbon with gold or silver metallic threads woven into it, in a wide range of colors. Sold in narrow and wide widths, by the yard, at fabric and notions stores and departments.

Monogram letters: Commercial embroidered cotton or rayon initials for appliqué. Made in several different sizes and colors. Sold at fabric and notions stores and departments.

Net: Stiff, transparent, cobweblike fabric, in a wide array of colors. Sold by the yard, in 35- to 45-inch widths, at fabric stores and departments.

Nylon fastening tape: Nylon closure for garments, with tiny invisible hooks that can be pressed together to form a temporary bond. Made in white, black, and tan only, under brand name of Velcro. Sold in ½-inch width, by the inch at fabric and notions stores and departments.

Paillettes: Large, shiny, metallic or plastic disks, like sequins, with a hole near the edge instead of in the middle. Made in one size only, in a wide array of colors. Sold in packages of 100, at fabric and notions stores and departments.

Pearls: Small to large round plastic beads with a pearllike finish, in white and pastel colors. Sold in strands, packages, or singly in the case of large ones, at craft and notions stores.

Persian yarn: Needlepoint and crewel yarn formed of three twisted strands, in an extremely wide range of beautiful colors. Sold by the skein or in individual strands, at needlework and yarn stores and departments.

Pinking shears: Scissors that make a decorative zigzag cut edge, used to prevent raveling of cut fabric edges. Sold at fabric and notions stores and departments.

Pipe cleaners: Flexible wire rods covered with chenille, intended for cleaning pipe stems; also used for crafts. Made in white and various colors. Sold at stationery, tobacco, dime, and craft stores.

Plastic wood: Synthetic filler that simulates wood when dry. Sold in tube or can, in various shades, at hardware, paint, and dime stores.

Polyester thread: Slightly stretchy synthetic thread for sewing modern stretch fabrics. Made in wide range of colors. Sold on spools, at fabric and notions stores and departments.

Purse handles: Made of plastic, leather, wood, or metal, in a wide range of colors and in several sizes and styles. Sold at craft, notions, and needlework stores and departments.

Ribbon: Lengths of narrow finished fabric in silk, cotton, velvet, vinyl, and other materials. Made in a wide range of colors, in many widths and patterns. Sold at fabric, trimming, dime, and notions stores and departments.

Rickrack: Decorative, zigzag-edged woven cotton trim, in a wide range of colors. Sold in packages of 3-yard lengths and ½-inch and 1-inch widths, at fabric and notions stores and departments.

Seam binding: Rayon binding for finishing the raw edge of a fabric. Made in a wide range of colors, in one size, ½ inch wide. Sold in packages of 3-yard lengths, at fabric and notions stores and departments.

Seam ripper: Pointed sharp instrument for cutting stitches. Sold at fabric and notions stores and departments.

Sequins: Small, shiny metal or plastic disks with a hole in the middle for attaching by thread to fabric. Made in a wide range of colors, in several different sizes. Sold at fabric or notions stores and departments.

Shellac: Clear, protective liquid for sealing raw wood and finishing craft projects. Sold in jars or cans, at hardware and paint stores.

Snaps: Two-part metal closures for garments. Made in two colors, black and silver, in several sizes, ranging from lightweight to heavy-duty. Usually available on a card containing several of one size. Sold at fabric and notions stores and departments.

Spray paint: Available in shiny or dull finish and in a wide range of colors. Sold in aerosol cans at hardware, paint, and some craft and dime stores.

Suede cloth: Napped cotton fabric simulating suede. Made in several colors. Sold by the yard, or fraction thereof, in 45-inch widths, at fabric stores and departments.

T-pins: Large T-shaped pins for holding macramé knots or securing wigs to wig stands. Made in one size only. Sold several to a package or by the box, at notions, craft, and dime stores and departments.

Tassels: Individual groups of decorative fringe, in a wide range of colors and several styles. Made of cotton, rayon, or silk. Sold singly, at fabric, notions, and upholstery supply stores and departments.

Tassel fringe or trim: Many tassels attached to one woven fabric heading; several styles and widths. Sold by the yard, at fabric, trim, and some upholstery shops.

Textile paints: Machine-washable paint (not dye) designed for coloring fabric, leather, or suede. Several colors available, which can be mixed to make other shades. (Acrylic paints may also be used for painting on fabric; in fact, I prefer them to textile paints.) Sold in jars, at art supply and craft stores.

Thongs: Long thin strips of leather; leather ski boot laces may be substituted. Made in a variety of colors, usually 45 to 60 inches long. Sold at shoe repair and craft shops.

Tracing paper: Transparent paper for tracing designs; thin typing or tissue paper may be substituted. Sold by the box or pad, 9 by 12 inches, at art, dime, and stationery stores.

Transparent thread: Clear, stiff, nylon thread for sewing multicolored fabrics. Sold on spools, in clear white and clear black, at fabric and notions stores and departments.

Trim: See *Ball fringe, Braid, Ribbon, Tassels,* etc.

Twill tape: Woven cotton utility ribbon, in white and black only. Available in ½-inch width, either packaged on a card in 3-yard lengths or by the yard. Sold at fabric and notions stores and departments.

Upholstery cording: Twisted soft cotton cord for weltings on upholstery. Made in white only, in several widths ranging from ¼ inch to almost 1 inch. Sold at fabric, upholstery supply, and notions stores and departments.

Vinyl: Shiny-surfaced, plastic fabric that wipes clean easily. Made in a wide range of colors and many different patterns. Sold by the yard in 72-inch width only, at fabric stores.

Wire: Metal used for attaching and stiffening. Made in several different colors, materials, and gauges (thicknesses). Sold on spools or by the foot, at hardware and craft stores.

Wool double-knit: Machine-made fabric with a

knitted look. Made in a wide range of colors and patterns. Sold in wide widths, 45 to 60 inches, at fabric stores and departments.

Wool fabric: Woven fabric made of 100-percent wool. Made in many colors, weaves, and patterns. Sold in wide widths, 60 to 72 inches, at fabric stores and departments.

Yarn: See *Knitting yarn, Persian yarn.*

Zipper adhesive tape: Press-on tape for holding a zipper in place before stitching. Prepackaged as a roll that can be used for many zippers. Sold at fabric and notions stores and departments.

Fabrics and Trims

If "Never sew unless you want to" is the main credo of this book, then "If you decide to sew, use only easy fabrics" is credo number 2. By easy fabrics, I mean those that are easy to work with, such as vinyl, felt, bonded knits, suede cloth, cotton, and low-pile fake furs.

All these are easy to cut, glue, sew, or bond together, and each comes in a wide range of vibrant colors and patterns, with the exception of felt, which comes in solid colors only. All have a substantial amount of stiffness or body, which makes it possible to avoid linings, interfacings, facings, and sometimes even zippers or buttonholes. Best of all, they are all relatively inexpensive to buy, come in wide widths, and are attractive as well.

Other materials are the keys to other shortcuts. You will be using ribbons instead of making belts and sashes; upholstery cording instead of covered drawstrings; frogs instead of buttons and buttonholes; and nylon fastening tape in place of hooks and eyes. You can buy crewel by the yard instead of stitching it yourself, use prepleated fabrics for pleated skirts, and work with bonded and quilted fabrics for both detail and body. Best of all, these items are not only time-savers but money-savers too, and they can give your garment that "special" look.

Easy-to-work-with means avoiding complicated prints and napped fabrics, both of which need matching and create waste. There are two exceptions to the no-nap rule: fake fur and suede cloth, which are too good to pass up. To determine the direction of the nap in these two fabrics, just run your hand lengthwise back and forth over the fabric and feel which way is smoothest. The correct way to use these fabrics is with the smoothest way, or the nap, going from the top to the bottom of your garment. You must lay out all your pattern pieces in this same direction.

To save time and trouble, you'll learn to work with sheets, towels, blankets, pillowcases, and the like, all of which come prehemmed and, in some instances, are already handsomely trimmed. To save money, think about becoming a shrewd shopper—you may be able to find these items at lower cost than similar fabric purchased by the yard. The smart shopper will watch the white sales and stock up on items she plans to use. Sometimes seconds can be your best buy, if the flaws are not obvious and you are able to work around them.

Watch for sales on fabric and trimming remnants and bolt ends, too. Wide trims can be joined together to create a magnificent fabric, for a fraction of the cost of buying a similar one ready-made. Watch for end-of-the-month and end-of-the-season clearance sales.

If your community has only expensive shops or a limited selection, don't be afraid to shop by mail-order catalog for basic ready-made clothing as well as supplies. You can easily customize mail-order clothes (note the Butterfly Hostess Jumper in Chapter 3 and the Lace-and-Denim Patio Ensemble in Chapter 4).

Sheets and blankets will become glamorous robes, hostess gowns, capes; pillowcases will become nightgowns; dish towels will become skirts; place mats will become children's smocks; curtains will become pinafores; and out-of-date clothing will come up-to-the-minute again. While you may not be able to afford an Yves St. Laurent, Bill Blass, or Vera original, you *can* afford to work with Yves's sheets, Bill's towels, and Vera's scarves and dish towels.

Felt is one of the easiest fabrics of all to work with. Unlike most other fabrics, it has no right or wrong side. Pattern pieces can be placed across the width instead of being laid out on the length without fear of throwing the entire garment out of line. Felt is economical, comes in 72-inch widths, and dazzles the eye with its wide range of brilliant and subtle colors, almost all of which coordinate beautifully with each other.

Felt is completely nonraveling and often does not even need to be hemmed. I especially like to use pinking shears to trim the edge of a garment made of felt. Felt takes to glue like a duck takes to water. It absorbs without soaking through, and a glued felt bond lasts forever. In fact, the only disadvantage to felt is that it must be dry-cleaned. But since white resin craft glue is dry-cleanable but dissolves in water, the combination of felt with glue is perfect.

Trimmings have been used for centuries to enhance fabrics. They are now available in such variety that they may be used alone or in combinations, to create such accessories as belts, chokers, collars, and hair ornaments. The Ruffled Eyelet Stole in Chapter 3, constructed entirely of trimmings, is a perfect case in point. So is the Scalloped Evening Belt in Chapter 5. The trims you will be working with for the most part are applied trims—applied by gluing, sewing, or bonding them to fabric. Sometimes, though, homemade trim is needed, such as buttons or flowers from felt. Directions for these can be found in Chapter 5.

Effective use of trims can make the difference between an ordinary wardrobe and a magnificent one. There truly are "fringe benefits" for the woman who learns that with the proper trimming, a run-of-the-mill garment can be turned into a custom-designed one that looks as if it cost two or three times its actual price.

Proper pressing is one of the real secrets of having garments look as if they had been made professionally. Note that I've said *pressing* instead of *ironing*. You will never iron garments as you are working on them; rather, you will press them. The difference lies in the technique. To iron a blouse you move the iron back and forth. To press a seam open or to press the creases out of a piece of fabric you are about to begin work on, simply touch the iron lightly to the fabric (which has been protected with a damp cloth) and then lift it up

before applying it to the next section. Proper pressing technique never involves pushing down on the iron for all you're worth!

Always make sure to have your iron set at the correct temperature for the fabric you are working on. If you are unsure as to how the fabric will react to the heat of the iron, test it on an area where it won't show, such as on an inside seam or along an edge of unfinished fabric.

For bargello, crewel, needlepoint, and other stitchery, pressing is vital to block the work into shape. Before pressing lightly, place the needlework face down on a folded heavy bath towel and cover the reverse side with a damp pressing cloth. Beaded or metallic fabrics, vinyl, and fabrics with nap should receive as little pressing as possible. If you do have to remove creases from these fabrics, always place them face down on a folded bath towel, cover with a damp pressing cloth, and set the iron for very low heat.

Finally, your steam iron can be helpful when applying trim around a curve, as the steam helps make the trim more pliable.

Some Tips and Shortcuts

When making garments for yourself, always try them on as you are working. When cutting, cut as much as possible at one time; do the pinning all at once, and the stitching all at the same time. Perhaps you'll spend one day just cutting out pieces for several projects and another day stitching or gluing the pieces together. It saves both time and trouble to proceed in this orderly manner. Press seams open as you sew, and remove all pins as you go.

If you must sew, go to your nearest pattern counter and study the "Jiffy," "Instant," or "Easy to Sew" sections of the pattern catalogs. These patterns have only a few pieces and not too many darts or zippers. They are designed for the beginner and for the seamstress in a hurry. The few actual patterns I give you in this book are so general that if you feel more secure using a commercial pattern instead, you can easily substitute one and avoid the slightly more complicated procedure of taking your own measurements in order to make your own pattern. The commercial patterns I use for the projects in this book are only of the easy variety.

Since I personally have never enlarged a graph pattern in all the time I've been crafting my own clothes, I have not included in this book any graph that must be enlarged. No matter how much I like an idea I see in a magazine, my time is too valuable to spend that way. Scaling up a graph can often take as much time as, or even more than, it takes to complete the entire project. If a pattern is called for, it's faster and easier to work from a well-made commercial pattern already in the right size.

Get more for your money by selecting a commercial pattern that provides several different looks or styles. When you find a pattern that works up well, make it in several different fabrics, trimmed in different ways. Always use the special patterns designed for knits when working with these fabrics; most are easy to sew and have no darts. Also use special polyester thread for sewing knits.

Sew only those items that are worth your time and on which you can save a lot of money. Try to avoid those that require a lot of fitting. Blouses usually can be bought at a reasonable price; they are too much trouble to make. A ready-made blouse, knit shirt, or sweater attached to a home-sewn skirt easily and inexpensively becomes a hostess or patio gown. And is it really worth the time, money, and effort to knit a sweater or coat? Consider crafting a coat like the one featured in the Fall Ensemble in Chapter 4, which looks hand-knitted even though only the sleeves are actually done by hand. Capes can serve the same purpose as coats, and ponchos as jackets, and both are far easier and more economical to construct. Save time making skirts by choosing a pattern that has no waistband or substitute grosgrain ribbon for the waistband.

Concentrate on separates, which are the backbone of a great wardrobe. Mixing and matching will make your wardrobe seem twice its size. Try working with unusual color and fabric combinations. A sensational wedding dress for a young bride can be made of unbleached muslin embellished with lavish embroidery. Don't be afraid to combine colors or fabrics that you've never tried together before.

Compliment Your Figure

Credo number 3 is "If your figure isn't perfect, make it look like it is." Rare is the woman whose figure and features are those of a Greek goddess. If you have a figure problem, the trimmings and accessories you choose can make or break your total fashion image. After all, there is no point in creating striking designs if you are unsure which designs suit you best. If you follow some basic principles for creating optical illusions to alleviate those trouble spots, you will make your figure appear more nearly ideal.

You should first analyze your own shape. Look at yourself in a mirror. Are you tall? Short? Skinny? Chubby? Big boned? Small boned? Just right? You, alone, must choose your own best fashion silhouette by learning which styles suit your shape, as well as your life-style and taste.

Here are some suggestions for ways to draw attention away from trouble spots by means of choosing patterns, fabrics, trims, accessories, and jewelry:

A short person should avoid two-piece outfits, which diminish figure height. Keep the hemline at about knee length. Fussy styles are permissible, but you certainly should not give the impression of an overly bedecked Christmas tree nor should you let your clothes overpower you.

A tall, thin person will appear more perfectly proportioned in full, but tailored, clothes. There should be a definite break or contrast at the waistline to take away that lanky image. Vertical stripes should be avoided at all costs. A pleasing hemline falls just below the knees.

Chubbies should think in terms of vertical stripes, or dark skirts or pants with light colored tops. Don't avoid belts; a loose belt (such as the Suede-Cloth Belt in Chapter 5) can actually be a help. The A-line silhouette is a good one for you, and so are pants suits. The idea is to draw attention away from your overall bulk by pretty, but not fussy, details. I like tricks such as placing unusual buttons (try the Felt Toggle Buttons in Chapter 5), off center to keep the viewer's eye off balance. Combining fabrics in two colors, as in a princess style with a light center and dark side panels, can be most flattering. (See *Diagram 1-AA*.)

Minimize a heavy bust by wearing a sleeveless tunic over a blouse or sweater. (See the Sporty Suede-Cloth Jerkin in Chapter 4.) A-line and princess styles are good for this figure problem, too. You want to create a straighter line, so avoid boleros and Empire waistlines, both of which focus attention on the bust. And watch out for your waist, too. If you emphasize it, it only makes your bust look bigger. Very wide sleeves and very flaring hemlines should also be avoided. Keep all major accents below the waist. Wear low, hip-slung belts. Have fun with pretty hemline details (see the New York Skyline Evening Skirt in Chapter 3) and clever accessories, such as a novel

DIAGRAM 1-AA

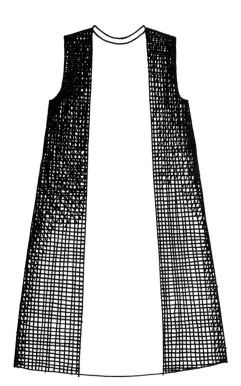

pocketbook (like the Pillow Tote in Chapter 6), or interesting shoes with unusual buckles.

A pear-shaped silhouette—heavy hips and bottom with a small bust—calls for details at the neck or bust. Use pretty scarves, collars, and necklaces, or try a big appliqué across the bust. Try anything that distracts the eye from the hip area. Pants suits hide a multitude of sins, and an Empire-style dress or coat is one of your best bets. You want a straight easy fit, with no dirndls or hip-hugger details. Remember to keep the major accents above your waist.

What I call the heart-shaped silhouette is the broad-shouldered woman who has a normal or small figure below the shoulder line. She can create an optical illusion by avoiding straight lines and choosing a full hemline. Any long, full skirt is excellent (the Patchwork Evening Skirt or the Bridge-Party Skirt in Chapter 3).

A long thin neck can be overcome by wearing turtlenecks, high collars, or scarves. Trim garments any place other than near the neckline to draw the eye away. (See *Diagram 1-BB*.)

The short-necked person should choose low collars and V-necks. Don't emphasize your neck area with chunky dangly earrings, and avoid turtlenecks like the plague.

Heavy thighs and knees can be disguised by the use of prints and by keeping hemlines a little longer than is actually fashionable. Long overblouses and tunics are good styles to hide those bulges.

Study the pattern categories that are found in the back of each company's pattern book and decide which one suits you best. In general, women's and misses' sizes are determined by the bust and hip measurements; men's and children's patterns by chest size. Patterns correspond pretty much to commercial dress sizes. For example: a 32 bust for a woman equals a size 10 dress; a 34 bust equals a size 12 dress; a 36 bust equals a size 14 dress, and so on.

Diagram 1-CC shows the basic shapes from which the vast majority of dress styles originate. Variations are achieved by using round, square, vertical, drawstring, halter, or other necklines and by using raglan, dolman, cap, set-in, or gathered sleeves in various lengths, or perhaps no sleeves at all. Skirt lengths can change the look of a garment, too. Dresses, skirts, and pants come in short

DIAGRAM 1-BB

(mini), medium (knee), midcalf (midi), or ankle or floor (maxi) lengths.

I've borrowed my fourth credo from a reference to cleaning out the refrigerator: "When in doubt, throw it out"; at the very least, set it aside until you determine whether it can be rejuvenated to fit your new craft fashion wardrobe. A closet full of clothes doesn't mean a thing unless the clothes are all ones you really wear. Your clothes must earn their own keep to stay in your closet. Thorough examination of what you have on hand can save many costly purchases.

Next, think about your life-style. What type of clothes makes you feel the most comfortable and secure? Do you like casual clothes? Do you like to get dressed up? Think of your favorite colors. Which colors make you feel happy? Which colors depress you? What colors are most becoming to your hair and skin tone?

Pull out anything hanging in your closet that you don't like to wear, that doesn't fit, or that you haven't worn in a year. Some of these garments can be revamped or rejuvenated, possibly by a procedure as simple as replacing buttons with frogs or adding a different belt. Perhaps some items can be taken apart to provide bits and pieces for making some of the projects in this book. Those clothes that are absolutely hopeless for you, although still serviceable, should be given to your favorite charity. And everything else should be thrown out.

But don't toss out any belts! They can be remade into pretty headbands (see Chapter 6) or purse handles; at least the buckles can always be reused. The buckle in the Diamond-Pattern Bargello Belt in Chapter 8 came from an old dress belt, for example.

DIAGRAM 1-CC

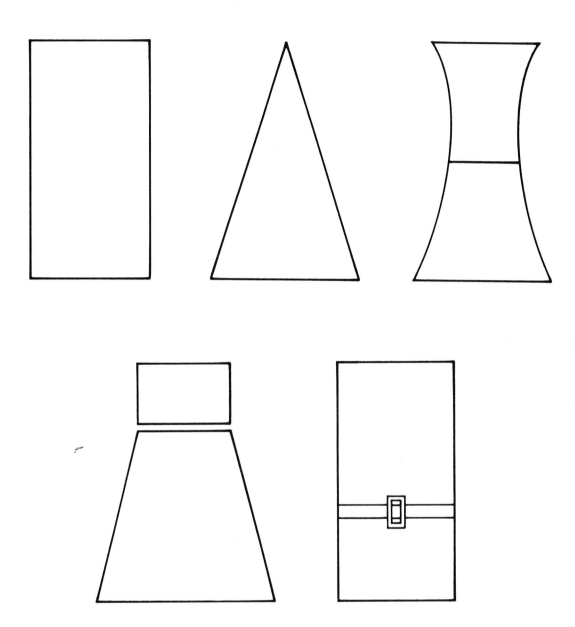

2
Use
the Craft-y
Approach

Here, in alphabetical order, are the most useful craft techniques you'll need to know, as well as practical hints and some simple, helpful diagrams. If a particular craft is especially interesting to you, you can learn more about it by consulting the craft books available at your library, book store, needlework or craft shop. If you want to brush up on your knitting or crocheting, or even learn these traditional skills from scratch, consult *The Complete Book of Knitting and Crocheting,* by Marguerite Maddox (Pocket Books), or any of the shorter guides to knitting and crocheting generally available at dime stores and other places where knitting supplies are sold.

Bargello: This needlepoint variation uses Persian yarn (a loosely twisted, three-strand yarn), a large-eyed, blunt-tipped needle, and single-mesh canvas. Bargello is four times as fast to produce as conventional needlepoint because it depends almost entirely on the Gobelin (pronounced "goblin") stitch, which is worked vertically, and occasionally horizontally, over several meshes of the canvas.

Don't let the name of the Gobelin stitch scare you! Just think of it as a simple running stitch covering three or four squares of canvas. The striking effect of bargello work, which lends itself to diamond and geometric designs, depends largely on the wide range of beautiful colors of Persian yarn. It is best to work with #10 or #12 canvas mesh, which have, respectively, ten or twelve squares of canvas to a linear inch. All supplies are available at needlework stores.

The bargello designs in this book are for simple projects such as belts and watchbands. Purchase canvas mesh by the yard (or fraction of a yard) and cut it to the desired size. Fold masking tape over the raw edges to prevent raveling. In an emergency, if it is necessary to join one piece of canvas to another before a project is completed, overlap the canvas about ¾ inch (or at least six meshes) and stitch through the two thicknesses of canvas as if they were a single thickness. Never pull stitches too tightly; bargello should be fluffy looking.

If you've never tried bargello, make up a sample before starting on a specific project. Insert threaded needle from the back of the canvas to the front, leaving a 1- or 2-inch tail of yarn on the wrong side, which you will secure by covering it with the next few stitches. Bring the needle up in mesh 1a, *Diagram 2-A1,* and, letting the yarn

DIAGRAM 2-A1

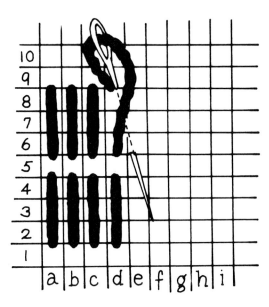

cover 3 vertical squares of the canvas, put the needle down through mesh 5a. Continue by bringing the needle up again in mesh 1b, down in mesh 5b, up in mesh 1c, and so on across the row. Work row 2 in a different color: needle up through mesh 5a, down in mesh 9a, up in mesh 5b, down in mesh 9b, and so on. For a different design, go up 2 squares or down 2 squares after 1 or more stitches (see *Diagram 2-A2*). No knots are used to begin or end yarn. Leave the end of the yarn hanging, and stitch right over it for about 1½ inches when beginning a new thread. To end a bargeilo row when you have run out of yarn, weave the yarn for about 2 inches through the back of your work and cut away the excess. To finish belts or watchbands, follow the individual project directions.

Beading on cloth: This beading procedure is the same as that used for applying sequins. First draw the beading design on paper, and then lightly pencil or chalk it in position on the garment. You might work a scroll design around a neckline or a straight band on cuffs; or you might highlight a part of the fabric's pattern.

Next, hand-stitch the beads in place, following your penciled outline. Work with nylon thread and a beading needle with a thin eye. Never work with more than 2 feet of thread, and never try to bead more than 3 inches with one thread. Beading can easily be damaged when you are putting it on or wearing it, and while it is easy to repair a 3-inch section, it is something else to have to rebead the entire top of a dress. Avoid heavy beading on the back of a garment—you don't want to sit on the beads. Large beads or sequins may sometimes be glued into place with craft glue, particularly in areas where they won't get much pressure, such as at the neckline or on the middle of a belt.

Bonding net "sewing": A new technological invention with exciting possibilities for needlework and crafts, bonding net is sold under at least two different brand names, Stitch Witchery and Poly Web. Both consist of cobweblike fibers, which melt under the heat of an iron to fuse one piece

DIAGRAM 2-A2

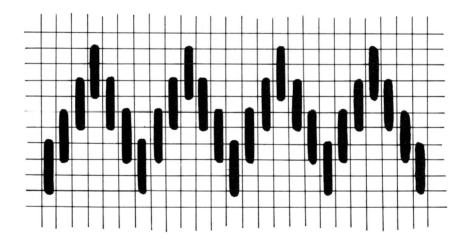

of fabric to another. This versatile aid can cut the time of hemming, trimming, or appliquéing to a matter of minutes. Place bonding net between the two layers of fabric to be joined and, following package directions, place a steam iron set at "wool" directly over the top piece for about ten seconds. The bond formed is both washable and dry-cleanable. Bonding net adds some stiffness or body to fabrics because it melts right into them. It is wonderful for use on hems, facings, trims, and appliqués, for making patchwork, and even for lengthening skirts. You can "sew" entire projects with bonding net—as I have done to make many of the projects in this book.

Casing constructing: Some projects require a casing, or "tunnel," of fabric through which you can run elastic or ribbon. There are two types of casings used in the projects in this book. The easiest is a skirt waistband casing. Turn fabric under ¼ inch if it is lightweight and nonraveling, press on the fold, and stitch or glue the ¼-inch hem in place. Then turn fabric under again the desired width of the casing and press on fold before stitching or gluing. If fabric is heavy or ravels easily, sew rayon seam binding or cotton bias tape to the raw edge of the fabric and then turn it under so that the seam binding or bias tape will not show; then fold under again the desired width of the casing. Press on fold and stitch or glue in place. The casing is now ready for elastic or cord to be inserted into it. Fasten a safety pin to one end of the elastic and push the pin through the casing, making sure the elastic at the open end is pinned or is long enough so that it doesn't escape your grasp. Stitch both ends of the elastic in place. If cord or ribbon is used, ends should be long enough to tie.

A second type of casing is used when the "tunnel" is to occur within the garment (not at a hem or waistband), as in a blouson-topped dress. Extra casing fabric (usually wide cotton bias tape) must be pinned in place on the inside or outside of the garment fabric, depending on whether or not you wish the casing to show. (On the "Knit" Purse in Chapter 6, I wanted the casing on the outside; on the Terry Towel Beach Shift in Chapter 4, on the inside.) Stitch the casing in place along both edges, removing pins as you go.

Feed the elastic or cord through the casing in the same manner as above.

Circle drawing: Some patterns call for cutting out a large circle or a half circle. For small circles use a compass and a sharp pencil. Larger circles require a different technique. Determine the diameter of the circle required. Divide by 2 to get the radius. Cut a piece of string a few inches longer than the radius. Tie the string around a pencil or piece of chalk and, holding the string taut, measure the exact length of the radius from the pencil or chalk. Mark this length on the string, and hold the string at this point while swinging an exact circle or half circle, which will be marked on the fabric with the pencil or chalk. (See *Diagram 2-B1.*)

DIAGRAM 2-B1

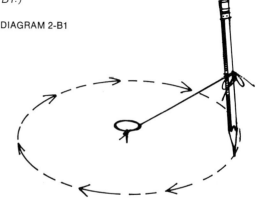

Embroidery substituting: Personally, I love to do embroidery, but it *does* take time. Often I can be satisfied simply with the effect of embroidery, which can be produced with an inexpensive product called Glow Writer, available at craft and dime stores. Another embroidery substitute is Glitter Magic, which is glitter mixed with glue in a single, pointed-tip tube for direct application to fabric. The same manufacturer (Walco-Linck Corporation of Clifton, N.J.) also produces a dripless glue pen, which permits fine-line writing and monogramming, over which glitter may be sprinkled. This pen can also be used for securing tiny beads sprinkled on fabric. All these are extremely durable and will survive twenty or thirty washings by hand or machine. They are easy for children to use, too.

Felt-tipped markers, available in bright colors, are another form of fake embroidery. Use permanent color, waterproof markers on garments you plan to wash.

Frog constructing: Frogs are soft, corded fastenings that give a decorative and expensive designer look to garments. It is possible to purchase ready-made frogs at a fabric store, but they are fairly expensive. Since frogs are such fun to make, you really should learn to make your own. They are made from covered cotton cording, which can be purchased by the yard at fabric and notions stores. Cording comes in a wide range of colors and thicknesses.

A frog has two parts, one a loop and the other a knotted button.

Work on a flat surface that will take pins, such as a macramé board (if you have one) or pillow, an ironing board, or a folded, heavy bath towel.

DIAGRAM 2-C1

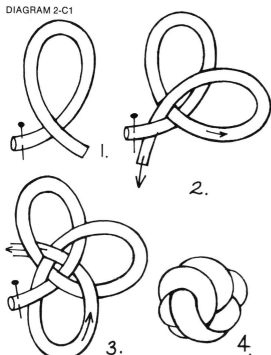

To make a medium-size frog, cut a strip of ¼-inch-diameter cording about 15 inches long for the button and another strip about 13 inches long for the loop. A few experiments with string will give you the proportions necessary for the particular size you want. Follow *Diagram 2-C1* for making the button part of the frog. Pin the ends of the cording to the rounded shape as shown in the diagram,

and add a drop of glue to secure. Let dry. The loop side of the frog is made in the same manner on the ends but is begun with a loop instead of the knotted button. Make sure the section with the raw ends of the cording falls *under* the loop or button. Fasten the ends with craft glue.

Hem constructing without seam binding: If you work with fabrics that do not ravel, such as felt or vinyl, you can often eliminate seam binding entirely by turning the hem up just as though it already had seam binding on it and then pressing and gluing or stitching it in place. For lightweight fabrics that might ravel (most cottons, some terrycloths), merely turn the edge under ¼ inch, press the fold, and machine stitch ⅛ inch from the fold. Then turn the hem up the desired amount, and pin and press it in place before gluing, bonding, or hand stitching to secure it.

Another way to avoid seam binding is to use pinking shears on firmly woven fabrics that are not likely to ravel (polyester double knits, flannels). Pinking shears give a decorative, yet useful, jagged edge. Turn up the hem as usual and press and pin it in place before stitching or gluing.

Macraméing: The art of making ornamental and decorative knots and fringe, pronounced "makra-may," has been around since the thirteenth century. Sailors created a wide range of macramé objects during their idle hours at sea, using readily available rope and the variety of knots they already knew.

Macramé is easy to learn and inexpensive to do. Smaller projects are portable, making it ideal pick-up work. Materials required are a macramé board, T-pins, and cord. There are only a few basic tips to remember:

1. Cords should be cut 8 times as long as the desired finished length, as you will always double them before working and the knotting uses up a great deal of cord.

2. To prevent cord ends from fraying, knot them or use a drop of white resin glue to secure end fibers.

3. If cords are very long, wind the ends into small bundles and secure them with rubber bands, leaving 2 or 3 feet free for working. Release about 2 feet of cord from the bundles as needed.

4. Pin knots in place on the macramé board or pillow as you work, moving pins as new knots are made.

There are only two basic macramé knots: the square knot and the half hitch and their many variations. For our purposes, learning the square knot and its variations is enough. Thus we will omit further references to the half hitch here. Tasséls can be used to finish off macramé (instructions following).

The usual starting knot is the lark's head. Pin a short cord horizontally across the top of the macramé board so that it is taut. This is the holding cord. (If you are making a belt, work the lark's heads right onto the bar of the buckle instead of onto the holding cord.) Fold each long cord (1 for each lark's head) in half. Push the folded end down behind the holding cord. Pull the 2 open ends through the loop and tighten to secure. (See *Diagram 2-D1*.)

DIAGRAM 2-D1

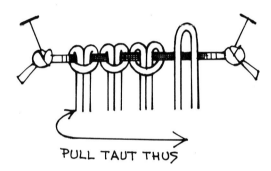

PULL TAUT THUS

Set up 2 lark's heads on your holding cord to try a square knot. You may already know how to tie this easy knot. It is always worked with 4 strands of cord. (See *Diagram 2-D2*.) Always hold

DIAGRAM 2-D2

the 2 center cords taut, and tighten the knot with the 2 outside cords. Do the square knot in these 4 easy steps:

1. Bring striped cord *under* 2 center white cords and *over* black cord, leaving a loop at the right.
2. Bring black cord over the two center cords and down through striped loop. Pull outside cords to secure.
3. Bring black cord *over* center cords and *under* striped cord, leaving a loop at the right.
4. Bring striped cord under center cords and up through black cord loop. Tighten knot by pulling on both outside cords.

Now set up 12 or 16 lark's heads on a holding cord or belt buckle (always work with multiples of 4 cords) and try a complete row of square knots. Work across in the same way as you did with the single square knot until the first row, 3 or 4 square knots, is completed. Pin knots after pulling them taut to keep row even.

On the second row make alternating square knots: Skip the first 2 and last 2 cords in the row, working with the next 4 cords just as you did in row 1. (See *Diagram 2-D3*.) On the third row return to the same pattern as the first row. The fourth row is the same as the second row. Continue alternating knots until the desired length of the project is reached.

DIAGRAM 2-D3

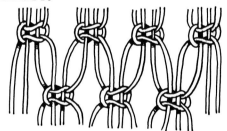

To end a macramé project, leave several inches of cord after the last row of knots in the pattern to make tassels. Knot the ends to a belt

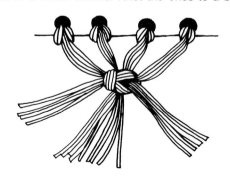

buckle or the like, or glue the last row of knots, let dry, tuck the ends into the back of the knotting an inch or so, and cut off, gluing cut ends.

Monogramming: My favorite way to monogram is to draw on scrap felt the initials I will be monogramming and then cut out the thickest part of the letter with manicure scissors, as shown in *Diagram 2-E1.* Draw letters freehand, or trace them

DIAGRAM 2-E1

from a magazine or newspaper. Now pin or glue these felt pieces into place on the article you wish to monogram and redraw the ends lightly with pencil or chalk on the actual garment. Don't be afraid to overlap or intertwine initials; it creates a more interesting effect. Now work satin stitch completely over each letter, chalk lines, and felt. The felt serves as padding to give your monogram a raised effect. Use embroidery floss in a color to contrast with the background fabric, but make sure the felt padding is the same color as the embroidery floss.

To work the satin stitch, thread an embroidery needle with embroidery floss, using all 6 strands, and insert needle from the underside of the fabric, as shown in *Diagram 2-E2.* Come up through the

DIAGRAM 2-E2

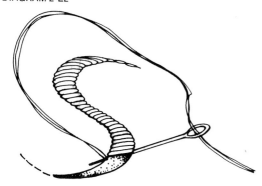

fabric, cross the letter, and go down again on the other side. Work over and over, so that the back looks the same as the front. Be sure to keep your stitches close together.

You can also purchase inexpensive iron-on monogram embroidery transfers to use as a basis for satin stitch. This will result in a flat monogram unless you add felt padding.

If you like, you can sew or glue inexpensive ready-made monograms directly onto a garment, and it is possible even to embroider over these.

Patchworking: Patchwork looks intricate but is not at all hard to do. Here are two methods of making patchwork:

1. Cut fabric patches the desired size plus ½ inch extra on all sides for seam allowance. Seam them together as shown in *Diagram 2-F1* to make a strip of fabric as long as the desired amount of

DIAGRAM 2-F1

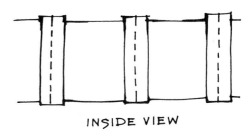

INSIDE VIEW

fabric required for a particular project. Press seams open. Make as many strips as required. Then seam strips together as shown in *Diagram 2-F2,* matching up seams. Press seams open.

DIAGRAM 2-F2

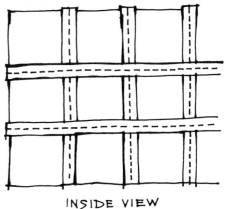

INSIDE VIEW

34

2. In this method the patches are overlapped and joined to a backing fabric or garment with bonding net. Patches of fabric that are likely to ravel should have raw edges folded under ¼ inch before bonding. Later, rickrack or other trim may be alternately applied to cover raw edges. (See *Diagram 2-F3.*)

DIAGRAM 2-F3

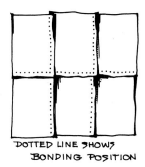

DOTTED LINE SHOWS
BONDING POSITION

Obviously the seam-together method is the only one to use with fabrics that might melt, such as vinyl.

Stitch-hole removing: Should you make an error in the construction of a garment, there are two easy ways to remove from the fabric the holes made by machine stitching. With a seam ripper or manicure scissors, gently open the seam you wish to redo and carefully remove all threads. Then press seam allowances flat with a steam iron and a damp pressing cloth. This method will work in the majority of cases. If it doesn't, use your fingers to stretch the fabric lightly in both directions around the holes. Work at right angles, both with and against the weave of the fabric, trying to pull the threads back into line. Finish by pressing with a steam iron and a damp pressing cloth. Let dry before restitching.

Tacking: Tacking is simply taking a few small stitches, one over the other, to secure one piece of material to another. It is always done with a regular sewing needle and a single or double thread, depending on how secure the article must be. For tacking plastic flowers on a hat, a double thread is definitely needed. For tacking a thin fabric facing or lining to the body of the garment, use a single thread.

Tassel making: Tassels are bunches of swinging fringe that hang from scarves, hems, drapery tiebacks, and so on. Although you can purchase them ready-made, they're very easy to make yourself in the color and yarn of your choice.

To make a tassel, cut a small piece of cardboard the length of the tassel desired. Wrap yarn or string around and around the length of the cardboard—the more you wind, the thicker your tassel will be. Cut a 4- to 5-inch piece of yarn and

DIAGRAM 2-G1

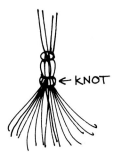

CUT OPEN

← KNOT

loop it through the top of the yarn on the cardboard, as shown in *Diagram 2-G1.* Tie tightly in a double knot but do not cut. Do cut across the bottom of the tassel, and remove it from the cardboard. Now take another short length of yarn and wrap it around the tassel about 1 inch down from the top. Knot it once or twice to secure it, and cut the ends, leaving them ½ inch long; push these into the top of the tassel, using the tip of your scissors. The yarn left at the very top of the tassel, which you did not cut away, will be used to tie the tassel to whatever it is going on. Tie securely and cut away excess yarn.

Topstitching: Topstitching refers to machine stitching that occurs on the right or top side of a garment and serves both a decorative and a functional purpose. Topstitching is begun very close to the folded edge of a hem or seam and should proceed in a straight, even line to ensure a uniform look. When several rows of topstitching are used, they should be parallel to each other. The presser foot on the sewing machine is the best guide for making even topstitched rows that are about ⅛ inch apart. Topstitching can be done with either a contrasting or a matching thread color.

Trim applying: Narrow trims (less than ½ inch) may be applied by gluing or by sewing by hand or machine. Wider trims may be applied in the same ways or by bonding net. Whether you glue, sew, or bond, conceal the raw edges of the trim by turning them under ¼ to ½ inch and pinning them to the fabric in the position desired. Remove the pins as you stitch or glue. To glue, apply an even coat to the back of the trim a few inches at a time, using the nozzle on the glue bottle or a small artist's brush to spread. Press the trim into place to secure it, and let it dry well. To stitch, follow the line where the trim has been carefully pinned in place. Narrow trims (¼ inch) should be sewn down the center; wider trims should be sewn along both edges. In order to blend as much as possible, thread color should either match that of the trim or be transparent.

To use bonding net, it's best to work with the precut bonding net strips, which are ½ inch wide. To apply exceptionally wide trims, bonding net by the yard is suggested. Cut net into strips the same width as the trim.

Turning right side out: It is frequently necessary, for such things as halter ties or bathrobe sashes, to seam a long, narrow strip of fabric on the wrong side and then turn it right side out. Here is the way to do it: After the fabric has been cut to the desired size, fold it according to project directions with right sides together. Stitch all raw edges about ½ inch from the edge, leaving an unstitched opening of about 3 inches at one end. With the eraser end of a pencil, or a yardstick (for a longer and wider strip), push the closed end back, through the strip, between the right sides of the fabric, and out the opening.

Another way to do this is by attaching a safety pin to the closed end of the strip and pushing the pin back through the strip, bringing the pin and attached fabric out through the opening. Press the strip flat, turning the open edges under ½ inch. Hand sew the opening together.

To make a neat job of it, pull out the corners with a straight pin so that they are sharp and not lumpy or rounded.

Instant Fashion Crafts

Here are a few of my favorite quickie fashion ideas, so simple that you won't need detailed directions for them. Not only will these ideas save you precious fashion dollars, but even more important, they may trigger some good ideas of your own.

☐ For a fast and easy beach hat, fold a square scarf diagonally, press, and stitch a straight line 1¼ inches in from the fold. Push a plastic headband through this casing.

☐ Make an instant turban by pulling both ends of a rectangular scarf through a wide belt buckle (the kind without a metal prong).

☐ Use a man's tie for a dramatic sash on a long skirt.

☐ Make your own patchwork fabric to use for sewing a man's necktie from a commercial tie pattern. Tie patches should be seamed together rather that bonded, as the bonding makes the fabric stiff.

☐ Use a clip-on cafe curtain ring to anchor a scarf around your neck. Fasten the clip to one end of the scarf and pull the other end through the ring.

☐ Wear scatter pins on the cuff of your blouse or sweater or, equally unexpected, on your shoulder.

☐ Trim plain plastic sunglasses by gluing beads, cording, or pearls to the frames. Trim ski goggles with a narrow band of real fur trim purchased from your fabric store. (I gave my sister, who has everything, a pair of mink-trimmed ski goggles one Christmas—it was her favorite gift.)

☐ Glamorize a dime-store hairbow by gluing on an edging of pearls.

☐ Make a chignon or hair-bun covering from a round, crocheted doily 8 or 9 inches in diameter and white elastic thread. Thread a needle with about 20 inches of elastic thread; knot the end of the thread around one of the crocheted holes on the outer edge of the doily. Take stitches in and out of the holes all around doily until you get back to the knot. Draw the elastic tightly to about 3 to 4 inches and knot to secure. Simply slip over hair-bun to wear, anchoring with a hairpin or two if needed.

☐ Use a door bolt from the hardware store to replace the clasp on a wood framed purse.

☐ For an instant hip-hugger belt, use a length of lightweight metal chain from the hardware store with a small combination lock as a clasp.

☐ Don't throw out broken jewelry and odd buttons. Recombine and restring beads for bracelets and necklaces, make button jewelry, and reuse all clasps and findings. Use white resin glue or epoxy to secure jewelry pieces together.

☐ To make drop earrings from a pair of ball-shaped, shank-type buttons in pearl or gold color, ½ to 1 inch in diameter, use pliers to open the shank on the back of the button and insert it through the little loop on a drop-type earring back. Close the shank to fasten. Repeat for the other earring.

□ Make a pendant by attaching several small or medium-sized ball-shaped shank-type buttons to the links of a plain gold metal chain in the same way.

□ Glue a pair of small buttons to a pair of cufflink backs, or glue a single button to a pin back. Use pliers to twist the shank off a domed button before gluing. White resin glue or epoxy are best. Brass and leather buttons are particularly effective when used in this way.

□ Wash a pair of dirty but still good sneakers, and dye them. Cut out tiny odd-shaped patches of felt and glue them on the sneakers. Trim around the base of the sneakers with glued-on decorative yarn or narrow braid.

□ Redye a pair of plain leather pumps with shoe dye. Purchase a metal stud kit and put studs around the heels.

□ Use two small (2-inch) drapery tassels and glue them to the throats of a pair of dress shoes. Match tassels to the color of shoes.

□ For a dressy belt, interlock two silk-tasseled drapery tiebacks.

□ A soiled flat envelope-style purse can be revitalized by gluing on alternating rows of beaded trim and velvet ribbon.

□ Dress up a ready-made bolero, using about 4 yards of wide gold rickrack and 2 yards of 2-inch-wide gold braid or other trim. Pin the rickrack in place

along front, bottom, and neck ½ inch in from edge; pin the 2-inch-wide trimming next to the rickrack with the edges touching but not overlapping; then pin another row of rickrack on the other side of the 2-inch trim. Stitch or glue the 3 rows in place, removing pins as you work.

□ Open the outside seams of a pair of narrow-leg slacks for 10 to 12 inches from the bottom. Cut a felt triangle 10 to 12 inches high by 8 inches wide at the base. Glue rows of ruffling to the triangle. Insert triangle into leg opening and sew to seam allowances.

□ Make a practical kitchen apron from a large open-weave dishcloth, gathered at one long side and attached to a length of ribbon.

□ Convert a plain sweater to a romantic pinafore sweater by sewing ruffling purchased by the yard to the armhole seam.

□ Trim a plastic umbrella by gluing ball fringe or embroidered trim around the edge.

□ Decorate synthetic silk or rayon umbrellas with iron-on transfers.

□ Make a halter by using a large square scarf at least 30 to 40 inches long. Fold one edge under 1¼ inches, press and sew to make a casing. Run a metal neck choker through this casing, and tie the bottom two corners in back.

CASING

BACK

□ Use designer sheets to create your own designer original from a commercial pattern. If you study the pattern pieces carefully, you can save yourself some work. Line the pieces up along the sides or the selvages of the sheet if possible. Place the bottom hemline along the wide hemmed top of the sheet if you are sure the hem will fall in the right place. (Make

sure your sheet has no top or bottom direction to the design.)

For a matching stole measure in both directions 1½ yards from the corner along the edges; draw a diagonal between the 2 end points and cut on this line. Hem or sew braid or other trim to the cut edge.

☐ Use a colorful plastic shower curtain as fabric from which to make a rain cape, using a commercial pattern.

☐ Use a twin blanket or an inexpensive lightweight quilted comforter to make a cozy winter bathrobe from a commercial pattern. You can color-coordinate it to your bedroom or bath, too. Save time by using the blanket bindings for the front openings of the robe.

☐ Avoid making belt loops on any bathrobe by attaching one part of a heavy-duty snap to the sash, and the other part to the corresponding part of the robe.

☐ Use the buckles and clasps from old sporty watchbands to fasten new macramé watchbands made in the square knot pattern.

☐ Cut the wide end from a man's tie to convert it to a tie for a young boy. Use the narrow end and overcast the raw edge.

☐ Use old terry cloth bath towels to make bath mitts for children. Trace around child's hand, add ½-inch seam allowance, cut out, and sew the 2 pieces together. Soap goes right inside.

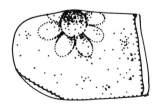

☐ Cut out iron-on patches in interesting shapes (like animals or cars) for a young child's worn-out pants knees.

☐ Use hand embroidery to add color or detail to a ready-made garment with a machine-embroidered or printed design. I use emerald green and variegated pink-red embroidery floss to highlight the leaves and flowers already machine-embroidered in brown on a darker brown suede-cloth vest. Or you could emphasize one strip of a plaid or an occasional polka dot.

☐ Use colorful felt-tipped markers to customize a black-and-white print fabric. Color in desired parts of design in the dominant color. Let dry completely. Add second, third, and fourth colors as you like, letting each dry completely before applying the next. (Make sure you use waterproof pens if the fabric will be washed.)

☐ Make a dickey and cuff set from an old blouse or skirt. Cut the cuffs off, leaving about 4 inches of sleeve attached, and hem the raw top edges. Cut off collar with about 4 inches of fabric attached and again hem the raw edges. Tuck under sweaters or body suits.

☐ An old turtleneck sweater can provide a dickey, too. Cut out desired shape and machine-stitch the raw edges to prevent raveling.

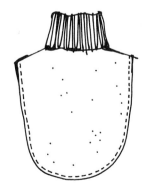

3
Festive
Fashions

Holiday-Dazzle Cocktail Dress

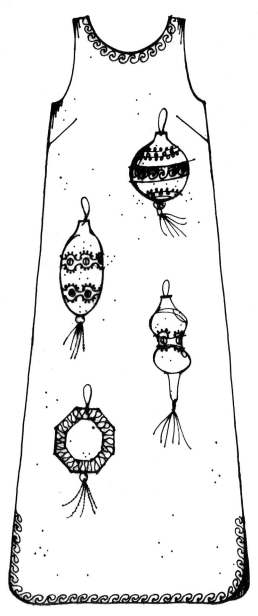

DIAGRAM 3-AA

This holiday-season evening dress looks as though it cost a fortune, but its actual cost is less than $12—even less if you already have leftover

scraps of fancy gold or beaded trims. You'll cause a stir at any holiday party when you wear this novel design.

MATERIALS

1 commercial pattern for long, sleeveless evening dress with opening at back

felt (length determined by doubling yardage on pattern to allow for lining), 72 inches wide

1 zipper, 16 to 20 inches long (depending on the commercial pattern specifications)

zipper adhesive tape

thread to match felt

compass

2 felt rectangles, 9 by 12 inches, in contrasting color to felt

2 felt rectangles, 9 by 12 inches, in second contrasting color

white resin glue

12 inches cording, ⅛ inch wide, in gold

1 spool metallic crochet thread, in gold

10 inches fancy trim, 1½ inches wide, in gold

8 inches gold and pearl trim, ½ inch wide

3 to 5 yards scroll braid (length depends on width of hem and neckline), ½ inch wide, in gold

1 hook and eye

1. Double the felt lengthwise and lay the pattern on it. Cut out 2 of each pattern piece (1 of each for the dress and 1 of each for the lining), but omit the facings. If there are any darts, sew them separately on the dress and the lining. The pattern pieces for dress and lining should also be sewed separately and then put together with wrong sides facing. (Although felt has no right or wrong side, consider the stitched sides of the darts the wrong side of the fabric.) Topstitch the lining to the dress at the neckline, armholes, and hemline after adjusting the length. Topstitch dress to lining on both sides of the back zipper opening, ⅛ inch in from edges. Insert the zipper into the neckline opening, attach with zipper tape, and stitch in place. Remove tape and press out all seams.

2. Follow *Diagram 3-A1* for all ornaments. Use a compass to draw and cut out a 5½-inch circle of contrasting color felt with a 1-inch tab at 1 end. On the same color felt, draw and cut out

DIAGRAM 3-A1

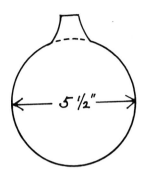

3. On the second square of contrasting color felt, cut out an oval about 7 inches long and 5 inches wide with a 1-inch tab at the top, as you did in step 2. On the same color felt, draw and cut out the last ornament, following *Diagram 3-A3*, remembering to make a 1-inch tab on the top of

DIAGRAM 3-A3

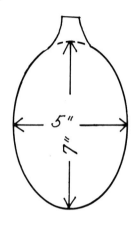

a circle, 7 inches in diameter. Follow *Diagram 3-A2* and draw intersecting lines to make an octagonal shape. Cut out along these lines.

DIAGRAM 3-A2

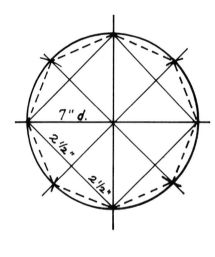

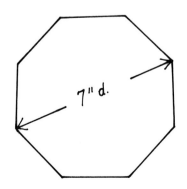

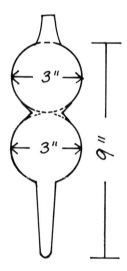

this ornament, too. This ornament should be 9 inches tall (not counting the tab) by 3 inches at the widest points.

4. Glue the ornaments to the front of the dress as shown in *Diagram 3-A4*, leaving 1 inch

DIAGRAM 3-A4

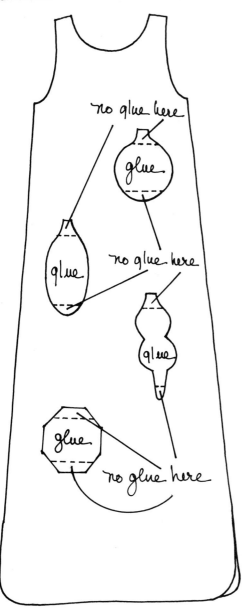

sels (see Chapter 2), 3½ inches long, winding the thread about 20 to 25 times. Glue the top of each tassel securely under the bottom center of each ornament, as shown in *Diagram 3-A5*.

DIAGRAM 3-A5

7. Glue the trims to the ornaments as shown in the *Diagram 3-AA*. Let dry.

8. Glue narrow gold scroll braid around the neckline and around the hemline. Let dry.

9. Sew a hook and eye just above the back zipper at the neck edge.

open and unglued at the exact top and bottom of each ornament.

5. Cut 4 pieces of gold cording, each 3 inches long. For each ornament, fold cord in half and insert raw ends ½ inch under the top. Glue to secure and let dry.

6. With the gold crochet thread, make 4 tas-

Silk Overskirt

DIAGRAM 3-BB

This unique accessory is made from two long rectangular silk scarves, cut in half, gathered, and attached to a waistband. It is particularly dramatic when worn over a simple wool or linen sheath or a jumpsuit; indeed, it looks lovely over almost anything.

MATERIALS

2 matching rectangular silk scarves, each approximately 12 by 36 inches

2 yards grosgrain or velvet ribbon, 1 inch wide, in any desired color

white resin glue (optional)

thread to match ribbon

1. Fold 1 scarf in half, bringing the short ends together. Pin or mark, and cut on the fold. Repeat for the other scarf.

2. By hand or machine, gather each of the 4 scarf pieces, making stitches ¼ inch in from the raw edges. Measure your waist and divide by 4.

Pull gathering thread until each scarf piece measures across top about 1 inch less than this measurement. (For example, if waist is 26 inches, gather each scarf piece to measure 5½ inches wide.)

3. Find the halfway point on the ribbon by folding it in half, bringing short ends together. Mark the point of fold and lay ribbon out full length. (If you are using velvet ribbon, lay velvet face down.) Pin a scarf piece close to the bottom edge of the ribbon on each side of the center, which you have marked. Pin the other 2 scarf pieces to the ribbon next to the first 2. (See *Diagram 3-B1.*)

DIAGRAM 3-B1

4. Sew by machine or hand, or glue the scarves in place on the waistband, removing pins as you go.

5. Fold the ribbon lengthwise to cover the gathering stitches of the scarf; pin in place, and sew or glue.

6. To wear, tie a short bow at waistline in front or back.

Lacy Pinafore Apron

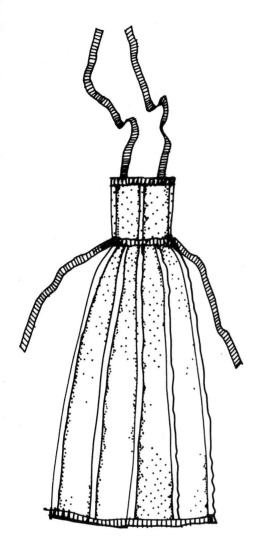

DIAGRAM 3-CC

This elegant long party apron is made of strips of wide lace trim seamed together instead of lace fabric, which is similar in appearance but much more expensive. You can often find these wide trims on sale, cutting the cost considerably. With a sewing machine you can complete the entire project in less than an hour; even by hand, it can be done in an evening.

MATERIALS

4¼ yards cotton lace trim, 6 to 7 inches wide, in any desired color
thread to match lace trim
5½ yards satin ribbon, 1 inch wide, in contrasting color

1. *Apron skirt:* Cut 4 strips of trim, each 30 inches long.

2: Pin the four 30-inch sections together lengthwise, overlapping each section by ¼ inch. (See *Diagram 3-C1.*) Sew down the center of each overlap, ⅛ inch from each edge. This forms the apron skirt.

DIAGRAM 3-C1

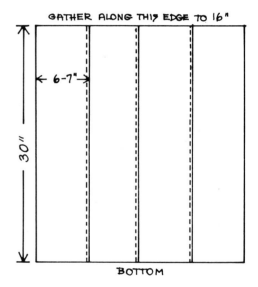

3. Gather across the top of the skirt by hand or machine, ½ inch in from edge. Pull the gathering thread until the top edge measures approximately 16 inches wide, and knot thread to hold gathers in place.

4. *Apron bib:* Cut 2 strips of trim, each 11 inches long.

5. Seam the 2 strips together as above, overlapping the sections by ¼ inch. The stitching is the center of the bib.

6. Fold apron skirt in half lengthwise and

mark center of gathered edge; unfold. Place bib over skirt section, overlapping ½ inch; bib stitching should meet center mark on skirt. Pin in place and sew together.

7. Cut 3 yards of ribbon for the waistband, including the ties. Fold in half, bringing short ends together, and mark waistband center on fold; unfold. Position ribbon so that waistband center is on apron center. Pin waistband and sew the top and bottom edges of the ribbon to secure it to the apron, ⅛ inch or less from each ribbon edge.

8. Cut ribbon to fit the bottom edge of the apron skirt plus ½ inch. Turn under and press a ¼-inch hem on skirt bottom. Pin ribbon on skirt so that bottom edge of ribbon is flush with skirt hem. Turn ends of ribbon (on sides of skirt) under ¼ inch. Sew in place.

9. Cut ribbon to fit the width of the top edge of the bib plus ½ inch. Turn under and press a ¼-inch hem at bib top. Pin ribbon on bib top so that top edge of ribbon is flush with top edge of hem. Turn ends of ribbon (on sides of bib) under ¼ inch. Sew in place.

10. Cut remaining ribbon into two 20-inch lengths for neckties. Attach ties to top of bib, positioning them 3½ inches in from sides and ½ inch down from top hem on the wrong side of the bib. Sew in place. (See *Diagram 3-C2*.)

11. To wear, tie at neck and waist.

DIAGRAM 3-C2

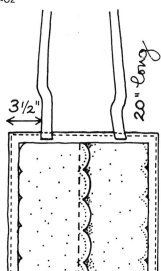

Instant Hostess Apron

DIAGRAM 3-DD

Using adhesive-backed craft trimming, this apron can be made in a jiffy for a special occasion. Although it won't withstand laundering, the trim can be peeled off the apron and used for another craft project. This design features a Christmas tree, but you can substitute a design suitable for any other occasion. If you have a solid-color apron on hand, you can use that, or you can make the net one described below in a matter of minutes.

MATERIALS

1 apron, in solid color, or net fabric, 20 by 36 inches, in any desired color, plus 2 yards grosgrain ribbon, 1 inch wide, in a contrasting color, and thread to match ribbon

1 package adhesive-backed craft trim, in holiday or other desired motif

1. *Net apron:* Gather fabric across the long side ¼ inch in from the edge, by hand or machine. Pull gathering thread until top measures about 18 inches wide, and knot to hold.

2. Fold ribbon in half and mark center point on fold; unfold. Fold apron in half lengthwise and mark center of gathered edge; unfold. Position ribbon to just cover gathering stitches, matching centers, and stitch in place very close to ribbon edge.

3. Cut craft trim to width of apron bottom;

remove the peel-off backing and press into place along the entire lower edge of the apron.

4. *Christmas tree:* Following *Diagram 3-D1,* cut the trim into one 6-inch length, two 2-inch

DIAGRAM 3-D1

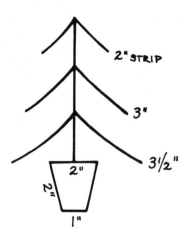

lengths, two 3-inch lengths, and two 3½-inch lengths. Press into place, positioning the 6-inch length vertically at the apron center beginning 6 inches below the waistband. Add the shorter strips for branches, as shown in diagram.

5. *Bucket:* Cut three 2-inch lengths and one 1-inch length of trim, and press into place as shown.

Butterfly Hostess Jumper

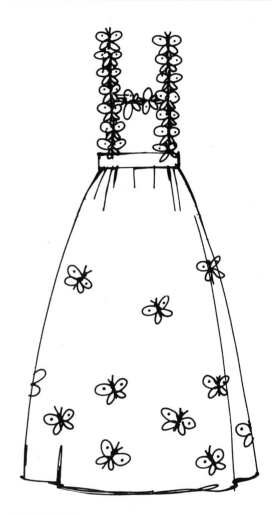

DIAGRAM 3-EE

I designed this jumper, wrote the directions, and asked my sister to make it up. She returned the completed project with a note: "This is a knock-out!" It's an easy way to perk up a mail-order or slightly worn long skirt. If you can't find butterflies, use flowers, stars, or embroidered trim in any other design that can be cut into units.

MATERIALS

1 long skirt, in any plain or lightly patterned or striped fabric (an old one can be used)

5 to 6 yards embroidered butterfly trim, 2 inches wide, in any desired color

⅛ yard felt, to match trim

white resin glue

1. Put on skirt, and measure from the waistband at the skirt front over your shoulder to back waistband. Cut 2 pieces of trim as long as this measurement plus 1 inch. Also cut 2 felt strips as wide as the trim to the same length.

2. Cut 1 piece of trim 10 inches long for the crossbar of the suspenders. Also cut 1 piece of felt 10 inches long and as wide as the trim.

3. Glue trim to felt backing cut in steps 1 and 2, making 3 pieces. On the crossbar, the butterflies will run horizontally, not vertically as they do on the strips. Let glue dry thoroughly.

4. Glue the crossbar to the suspender straps about 8 to 10 inches from the bottoms of the straps, or at the fullest part of the bust; the raw edges of the crossbar should lie ½ inch under each of the 2 straps.

5. Tack the suspenders securely to the inside of the skirt waistband at both front and back, with the raw edges of the straps ½ inch under waistband.

6. Take the remaining trim and cut it apart into separate butterflies. (This type of trim is designed to be cut apart; any raveling that may occur will be so minimal that binding the edges is unnecessary.)

7. Apply a dot of glue to the back of each butterfly and scatter the butterflies at random over the front of the skirt and along the hem of the back of the skirt. Avoid putting the butterflies high on the back of the skirt where they can become wrinkled when you sit down. Let dry thoroughly.

Family-Tree Sweater

DIAGRAM 3-FF

Make this glamorous sweater for a doting grandmother, or adapt the idea to recall the names of places you've visited, the streets in your town, or whatever else you wish, using diamonds, squares, or circles instead of hearts.

MATERIALS

1 sheet tracing paper

⅛ yard felt, in contrasting color to sweater, or 3 or 4 felt rectangles, 9 by 12 inches, all in 1 color

pinking shears (optional)

1 tube Glitter Magic, in gold

white resin glue

1 long-sleeved cardigan sweater (an old one may be used), in any desired color

3½ to 4 yards metallic trim, ½ inch wide, in gold

1. Trace heart shape in *Diagram 3-F1* and cut out. Pin this pattern to felt and cut out the desired

DIAGRAM 3-F1

Peasant-look Evening Skirt

DIAGRAM 3-GG

number of hearts, using regular scissors or pinking shears.

2. With Glitter Magic, write the names of family members, 1 on each heart. Let dry flat for several hours.

3. Glue hearts at random over the front and sleeves of the sweater. If the family is very large, the hearts may also be placed on the back of the sweater.

4. Glue gold metallic trim around the neckline and on either side of the buttons on the front opening, in 2 rows, ½ inch apart. Stretch sweater slightly as you glue so that it won't pucker the trim when it dries. Let dry completely.

This softly gathered skirt is most effective when it is made in an unusual color combination and worn with a coordinating-color sweater, turtleneck top, or body suit. I made it in hot pink and orange, two of my favorite colors, but you might try lavender and blue, green and navy, or any other striking combination.

MATERIALS

1½ yards wool or cotton double-knit fabric, 60 inches wide, in a solid color

2¾ yards embroidered rayon or cotton trim (for wool double-knit use rayon trim; for cotton double-knit, use cotton trim), in contrasting color

polyester thread to match both fabric and trim

3 yards grosgrain ribbon, 1 inch wide, to match predominant color of trim

1 package rayon seam binding, to match fabric

1. Fold fabric exactly in half lengthwise so that selvage edges meet evenly. Measure length from your waistline to your ankle and add 8 inches. Cut across both layers of folded fabric to this measurement. Now cut from top to bottom exactly through the fold. You should now have 2 pieces of fabric, each 30 inches wide and as long as your waist-to-ankle measurement plus 8 inches.

2. With right sides facing, pin and then seam the 2 pieces of fabric together on both sides, ½ inch from edges, leaving 2½ inches open at the top of each side seam to make casing in step 3. Gently stretch the fabric as you stitch so that the seams will not pucker, or use zigzag or other stretch stitch. Remove pins as you sew. Press seams open with steam iron set for wool or cotton, depending on the fabric. Fold the 2½-inch open seam edges back ½ inch and tack in place by hand on both sides. (See *Diagram 3-G1*.)

3. Turn the top edges of the skirt under ¼ inch, press, and stitch in place. Turn them down again 1 inch, press, and stitch in place at bottom edge to form casing. Leave casing ends open so that ribbon can be run through later. Do not insert the ribbon yet.

4. Turn skirt right side out, and lay it out flat on a table. Pin embroidered trim in place on the front of the skirt to form the apron panel, as shown in *Diagram 3-G2*. Miter the corners (fold on the diagonal) for a neat sharp edge. The apron panel runs 29 inches down from just below the casing stitching at the waistline, and the 2 parallel bands of trim are 13 inches apart.

5. Machine-stitch trim, using thread in the color of the trim and removing pins as you go. Stitch both sides of the trim and turn the top ends (at the waistband) under ¼ inch to avoid a raw edge. Make sure not to stitch over the casing.

6. Cut the grosgrain ribbon in half. Feed 1 half through the front casing of the skirt and 1 half through the back casing.

7. Stitch rayon seam binding to the bottom

DIAGRAM 3-G1

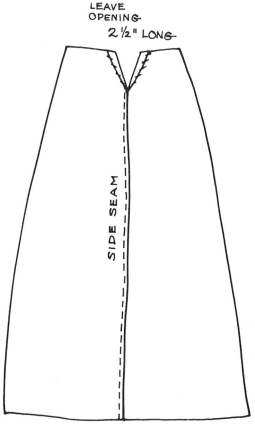

DIAGRAM 3-G2

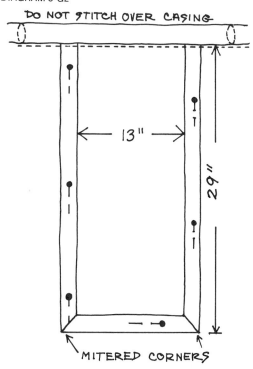

edge of the skirt and turn up hem the desired amount (4 to 5 inches). Press and pin the hem in place.

8. Hand-stitch the hem, using thread to match skirt. Remove pins as you work.

9. To wear, tie skirt at each side of the waist with a bow and streamers.

New York Skyline Evening Skirt

DIAGRAM 3-HH

This design is among my favorites. I live fifteen miles from New York City, and on a clear evening I can easily see the skyline. Although the skirt can be done in a pastel shade with a dark skyline, it is most dramatic in black and white. Wear it with a plain long-sleeved pullover or knit top so as not to distract from the skirt itself. The same commer-cial pattern can also be used for the bridge skirt in this chapter.

MATERIALS

1 commercial pattern for long A-line wrap-around skirt with tie in back
felt (length determined by yardage on pattern), 72 inches wide, in white or black
thread in black and white
2½ yards grosgrain ribbon, 1½ inches wide, to match smaller piece of felt
brown wrapping paper, equivalent in size to 2 sheets newspaper
¾ yard felt, in white or black to contrast with skirt
white resin glue
nylon fastening tape or 2 hooks and eyes

1. Lay out and cut skirt from felt, following pattern directions; assemble, pressing seams open. If the skirt has a waistband, use grosgrain ribbon instead. If the skirt pattern does not call for a waistband, add ribbon to skirt top—the contrast of the ribbon against the felt is important to the design. To make the waistband, cut a ¾-yard piece of ribbon and set aside. Pin remaining ribbon in place to top of skirt so that it is flush to the point where skirt wraps inside. Leave a long end hanging at the other, outer, end of the skirt waist. Topstitch top and bottom of ribbon in place

DIAGRAM 3-H1

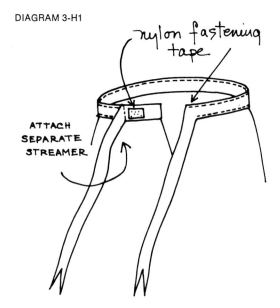

nylon fastening tape

ATTACH SEPARATE STREAMER

at top of skirt. Sew shorter piece of ribbon to waistband at the point where overlap ends. Tie 2 long ends into a bow with streamers when wearing. Sew hooks and eyes or nylon fastening tape as shown in *Diagram 3-H1*. To finish the hemline of the skirt, turn under ½ inch and press. Topstitch it in place with 2 parallel rows of machine stitching in thread to match skirt.

2. On brown wrapping paper, pencil in a skyline. Follow *Diagram 3-H2,* but do not try to enlarge this diagram accurately. The buildings can be any shape you desire; there is no need to enlarge a complicated graph. Just keep the heights of the buildings under 11 inches and make the paper pattern about 30 inches long. Make 1 building taller than the others, to represent the Empire State Building. You will be repeating the same 30-inch section about 3 times around the bottom of the skirt, depending on the skirt width.

3. Pin the paper pattern to the contrasting strip of felt across the 72-inch width and cut out the buildings. Repeat as many times as necessary to make enough pattern designs to go around the bottom of the skirt. Pin and glue the pieces in a continuous row, just above the top row of top-stitching on the hem. Remove the pins as you glue. Let dry completely, with the skirt opened out flat.

4. For windows, cut small rectangular shapes about 1 by ½ inch from felt scraps the same color as the skirt itself and glue them at random onto the buildings, as shown in the project illustration. You will need 40 to 50 windows in all.

5. Leave skirt flat until completely dry. Press lightly with a steam iron and pressing cloth before wearing.

DIAGRAM 3-H2

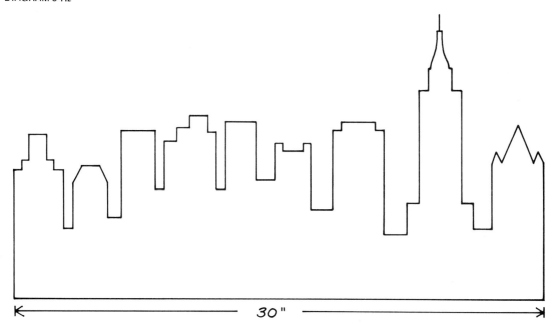

30"

Bridge-Party Skirt

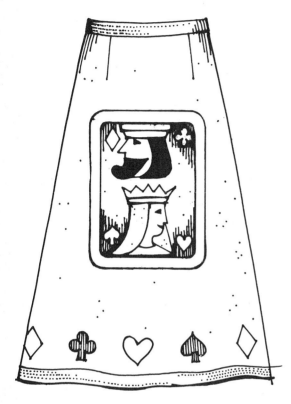

DIAGRAM 3-II

The effectiveness of this design, created especially for at-home evening bridge parties, depends on your choosing a vibrant color for the skirt. Try yellow, orange, lime, or shocking pink. The commercial pattern is the same as the one used to make the New York Skyline Evening Skirt.

MATERIALS

1 commercial pattern for long A-line wrap-around
    skirt with tie in back
felt (length determined by yardage on pattern), 72
    inches wide, in any desired color
thread to match skirt and 1 contrasting color
1 felt rectangle, 12 by 15 inches, in white
1 felt rectangle, 12 by 15 inches, in contrasting color
5 felt rectangles, 9 by 12 inches, 1 each in white,
    yellow, black, and 2 other contrasting colors
1 sheet tracing paper
white resin glue
3 inches nylon fastening tape

1. Lay out and cut skirt from felt, following pattern directions, allowing for 1-inch hem only; assemble, pressing seams open. If skirt pattern has a waistband, follow directions and add it.

2. Before finishing hem, try on the skirt and mark the waistline at the point where the skirt overlaps. Sew nylon fastening tape to matching flaps of the waistband, or skirt top, at this point. Turn hem up 1 inch and press in place. With contrasting thread, topstitch all around hemline, starting ⅛ inch from bottom fold. Work 6 separate parallel rows of machine topstitching up the hem, ⅛ inch apart.

3. Cut white felt rectangle to measure 11 by 15 inches, and round off the corners so that it resembles a playing card. Trim other 12- by 15-inch felt rectangle to measure 9 by 13 inches and round off corners. Center this piece on the white one so that there is an even margin of white showing all around, and glue.

4. On tracing paper, trace king and queen from *Diagram 3-11,* and the 4 small card suit symbols from *Diagram 3-12.* Cut out and pin to the remaining felt rectangles, choosing colors as you like. However, the king's hair should be black and the queen's hair yellow; the 4 symbols should each be a different color. Cut out all the felt shapes. Assemble the appropriate pieces to form the heads of the king and queen, positioning them in the center of the playing card shape, and glue in place. Glue the 4 card suit symbols to the corners of the playing cards, 1 in each corner. Let dry thoroughly.

5. Glue completed playing card to the center front of the skirt, placing the lower edge of the card about 11 inches up from the hemline. Lay skirt flat until dry.

6. Cut enough of the large felt card suit symbols *(Diagram 3-13)* to go around the hemline of the skirt, in 4 colors as before. You will need about 14 to 16 cutouts. Position them around the hem-

line approximately 6 inches apart, alternating the
4 different colors. Glue in place.

    7. Lay skirt flat until dry. Press with a steam
iron and pressing cloth before wearing.

DIAGRAM 3-I1

DIAGRAM 3-12

DIAGRAM 3-13

Patchwork Evening Skirt

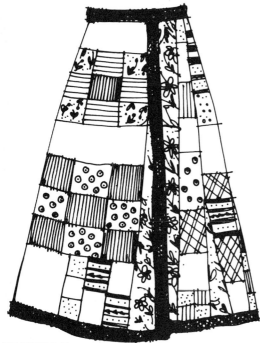

DIAGRAM 3-JJ

The patchwork quilt from which I made this skirt was in ragged shape when I found it at a rummage sale. I carefully separated the quilt from its lining and washed and ironed the patchwork, delighted to find that although it was hopeless to repair as a quilt, there was a considerable amount of undamaged fabric. So I made this skirt. I have since picked up three more old worn quilts at bargain prices and plan to make an entire patchwork wardrobe from them. If you can't find old patchwork at prices you can afford, make your own from leftover fabric scraps, following the directions in Chapter 2. Try using unusual combinations of fabric; for example, scraps of corduroy, cut velvet upholstery samples, and satin.

MATERIALS

1 old patchwork quilt or amount of patchwork fabric called for in commercial pattern for long A-line wrap-around skirt

1 commercial pattern for long A-line wrap-around skirt

3¼ yards firmly woven cotton, 36 inches wide (for lining)

thread to match dominant color of patchwork and lining

4 yards decorative trim, 2 inches wide, to contrast with patchwork

2 or 3 sets of hooks and eyes or nylon fastening tape

1. To reuse an old patchwork quilt, carefully separate the patchwork from the quilt lining. If necessary to cut through the quilting stitches, do so carefully so as not to tear the top. Discard the lining and padding if there is any. (If the quilt lining is in good condition, open 1 seam, remove padding, and follow steps 2 through 6 below, handling both layers of fabric together and omitting separate lining.)

2. Launder patchwork by hand if it is cotton or dry-clean (use the self-service machines) if it is silk or velvet. Dry it by hanging it on a clothesline, not in a clothes dryer. Press the patchwork with iron set at the correct temperature for fabric type, using a damp pressing cloth.

3. Using a commercial pattern, lay out the pattern pieces on the patchwork and cut out. Plan your skirt so that the center of the patchwork pattern, if there is one, or the best portion of the fabric comes at the front center of the skirt. Use the same pattern pieces to cut lining.

4. Follow pattern directions for assembling skirt. If directions for lining are not included, make up the lining following same directions as for skirt, but remember to put the wrong side of the patchwork against the wrong side of the lining before pinning and topstitching it in place, around waist and sides, ⅛ inch from edge. Omit facings. Press all seams. Insert lining before adding waistband, if there is one. Hem lining separately from the skirt lining so that the skirt will hang evenly. The lining hem may be done by machine as may the skirt hem, since the trim will cover the stitching.

5. Pin and machine-stitch the trim around the waist, down the front or overlapping edge, and all along the bottom over the hem-stitching. Remove pins as you go.

6. Try on skirt. Sew 2 or 3 hooks and eyes where skirt fastens at waistline, or use nylon fastening tape.

Ruffled Eyelet Stole

DIAGRAM 3-KK

This romantic design is both feminine and practical, as it protects bare shoulders from the drafts of summer air conditioning. It's striking when worn with a black dress and lovely with "ice cream" pastels, too.

MATERIALS

1¼ yards net fabric, in white

4 yards flat embroidered eyelet trim, 6 to 7 inches wide, or 2¾ yards pregathered trim

thread to match trim

3½ yards velvet ribbon, 1¼ inches wide, in black or other color

white resin glue

1. Fold net so that doubled piece measures 8 by 44 inches, and cut away excess. Cut away triangular pieces at corners. (See *Diagram 3-K1.*)

DIAGRAM 3-K1

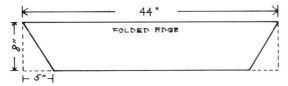

2. Measure and cut 2½ yards of flat embroidered eyelet trim. By hand or machine, gather across top ¼ inch from edge and pull gathering thread to make piece 1½ yards long. For pregathered trim, measure 1½ yards along gathered edge, and cut.

3. Gather remaining 1½ yards of flat trim, pulling thread to make 1¼ yards, in the same manner. For pregathered trim cut 1¼ yards.

4. Pin the shorter gathered piece to the top or longer (folded) edge of the net. Adjust the gathers evenly to fit the fabric, repinning if necessary. Sew in place along edge.

5. Begin pinning 1 end of the longer gathered piece at 1 top corner of the net and follow the shape, curving the trim, so that the bottom edge overhangs the side and lower (folded) edge of the net. The horizontal part of the trim should be about 5½ inches below the first row so that the top row of trim will cover the stitching of the second row. (See *Diagram 3-K2.*) Carry trim up to the other top

DIAGRAM 3-K2

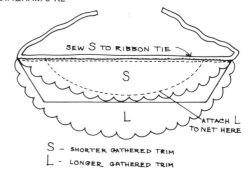

S — SHORTER GATHERED TRIM
L — LONGER GATHERED TRIM

corner. Be sure to adjust the gathers before stitching.

6. Cut an 80-inch length of velvet ribbon, long enough to cover the top edge of the stole plus enough for 18-inch ties on each side of the front. Fold ribbon in half and mark center point on fold; fold stole in half and mark center similarly. Match centers and pin ribbon to top of stole. Sew or glue in place.

7. Cut a second piece of ribbon, 44 inches long, and glue to the inside of the center section of the first piece of ribbon.

8. To finish off the front of the stole, turn the raw front side edges of both eyelet rows under ¼ inch and hand-stitch.

9. To wear, tie velvet bow in front.

Gypsy Shawl

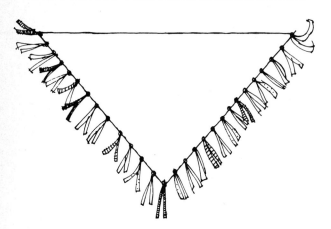

DIAGRAM 3-LL

Rayon seam binding in a riot of pretty colors masquerades as much more costly silk ribbon to trim this stole. For a cool night, a warmer wrap could be made from felt instead of crepe.

MATERIALS

1 square yard crepe or any other soft fabric, such as jersey or a light knit, or 1 ready-made triangular stole, in any desired fabric and color
thread to match fabric or white resin glue
paper punch (optional)
2 packages each rayon seam binding, in lavender, rose, orange, purple, yellow, bright pink, and green

1. Fold fabric diagonally into a triangle with right sides of fabric facing. Stitch or glue around the open edges, leaving about 3 inches open on 1 corner. If you use glue, let dry flat. Trim the seams if stitched.

2. Turn stole inside out through the 3-inch opening. Hand-stitch or glue the opening to close the triangle. If you use glue, let dry. Press the stole flat, using a steam iron set for synthetic or rayon fabric.

3. Using a paper punch or the pointed end of a scissors, pierce a tiny hole every 2 inches around the 2 short sides of the triangle, ½ inch in from the edge. (See *Diagram 3-L1.*)

DIAGRAM 3-L1

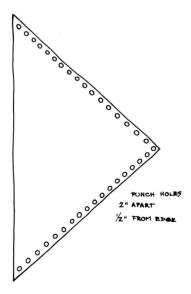

PUNCH HOLES
2" APART
½" FROM EDGE

4. Remove seam binding from packages and press to remove creases, using a steam iron set for synthetics or rayon.

5. As you work the following steps, cut the seam binding into 14-inch lengths.

6. Fold a strip of seam binding in half so that it measures 7 inches, and push the folded ends through the first hole along 1 edge of the stole.

7. Put the cut ends through the loop formed by the fold and pull to secure, as shown in *Diagram 3-L2.*

DIAGRAM 3-L2

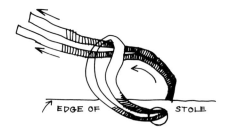

EDGE OF   STOLE

8. Repeat, alternating the 7 colors of seam binding, around the edges.

Fun Fur Capelet

DIAGRAM 3-MM

Because of today's concern for the preservation of wild animals, it has become more of a status symbol to wear fake fur than real. Choose one of the synthetics that look as fantastic as the real thing to make this luxurious capelet.

MATERIALS

¾ yard fake fur fabric
white resin glue
¾ yard felt, to match fake fur fabric
compass
3 by 3 inches foam rubber, ½ inch thick (buy ¼ or
    ½ yard at the dime store and use the remainder
    for other projects)
thread to match fur
1 large hook and eye

1. Cut out capelet, following *Diagram 3-M1,* from the fake fur fabric. With right sides together, seam the 2 pieces together by hand or machine where indicated.

DIAGRAM 3-M1

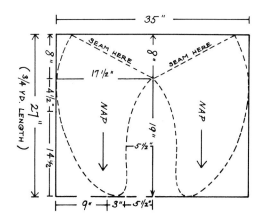

2. To hem, turn fabric under ½ inch all the way around, and glue lightly to secure. Let dry completely.

3. Cut felt lining for the capelet ¼ inch less all around than the hemmed size of the fake fur. Glue the inside edge of the lining to the wrong side of the capelet, covering all the hemmed, glued edges of the fur. (Just glue all around for about ¼ inch in from edge of felt lining.) Let dry completely.

4. Use compass to measure a 3-inch circle from the foam rubber; cut out. This will be the filler for a button. Use compass to measure a 4-inch circle from a piece of the fake fur fabric; cut out.

5. By hand, gather the fur circle ¼ inch in from the edge; do not cut off thread. Insert the foam rubber circle and pull thread tightly to close the fur circle around the foam rubber. Knot to secure. Sew this large button to the front of the stole.

6. Sew a large hook directly under the button to the felt lining of the capelet. Sew eye to the corresponding point on the outer (fake fur) side of the capelet.

Holiday Overblouse

DIAGRAM 3-NN

Although this blouse looks somewhat like a poncho, the concealed separation under the arms gives it a slightly more fitted shape. I designed it with a Christmas tree motif to wear over a turtle-

neck sweater and pants at holiday time, but if you wish, you can change the color scheme and design for wearing at other seasons of the year.

MATERIALS

1 felt square, 36 by 36 inches, in red

4 yards large ball fringe, to match large piece of felt

¾ yard small ball fringe, in same color

1 package bonding net (you'll need only about 10 inches)

brown wrapping paper, equivalent in size to 1 sheet newspaper

1 felt square, 9 by 12 inches, in green

white resin glue

3 inches metallic trim, ¼ inch wide, in gold

1 package paillettes, in assorted colors

1 tube Glitter Magic

1. Fold the large piece of felt in half diagonally and then in half again to form a 4-layered triangle, and cut out neckline as shown in *Diagram 3-N1.* Unfold.

DIAGRAM 3-N1

CUT AWAY SHADED AREA

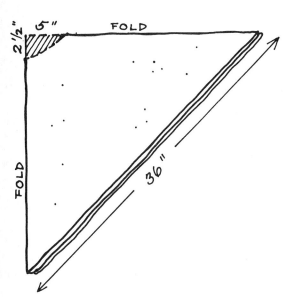

2. Glue large ball fringe around the 4 sides of the felt.

3. Glue the small ball fringe around the

neckline. Cut away excess fringe and save for another project.

4. Fold overblouse diagonally so that it forms a triangle. With bonding net, join the front and back underarm 12 inches below and parallel to shoulders, as shown in *Diagram 3-N2.*

DIAGRAM 3-N2

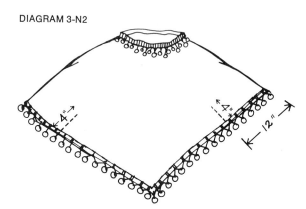

5. Draw a pattern on the wrapping paper for the Christmas tree and bucket, following *Diagram 3-N3;* cut out. Pin the pattern to the green felt square and cut out.

DIAGRAM 3-N3

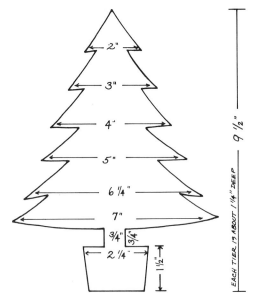

ENLARGE AND CUT OUT

6. Glue tree to the front center of the over-blouse. The top of the tree should be about 7 inches down from the center of the neckline.

7. Glue gold metallic trim to the top of the bucket that holds the Christmas tree. (See *Diagram 3-N4.*)

DIAGRAM 3-N4

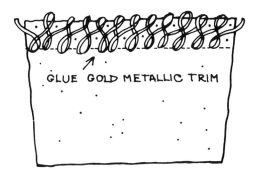

8. Glue the paillettes to the ends of the tree branches and scatter additional paillettes (about 25 in all) over the tree.

9. With Glitter Magic, put in wavy lines across the branches of the tree, write *Noel* across the bucket that holds the tree, and put a star at the top of the tree.

Ruffled Wrap-around Skirt

DIAGRAM 3-OO

I began this skirt at 3:00 P.M. to wear to a dinner dance that evening. It took less than two hours to finish, and it got more compliments than any other garment I've even worn. It looks especially striking when done in a bold-patterned fabric, and thanks to the elasticized waistband, one size fits all. If you're really in a hurry, substitute 2-inch-wide preruffled eyelet edging for the handmade ruffles and buy ½ yard less fabric.

MATERIALS

2⅔ yards cotton fabric, 36 inches wide

thread to match cotton

2 yards cotton batiste, 45 inches wide, in similar color (for lining)

1 package no-roll elastic, ½ inch wide

4 sets hooks and eyes

1. Unfold skirt fabric and lay it out flat. Following *Diagram 3-O1,* cut 2 pieces; the first, 36 by 36 inches; the second, 24 by 36 inches. Fabric

DIAGRAM 3-O1

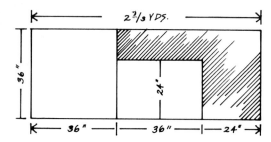

DIAGRAM 3-O2

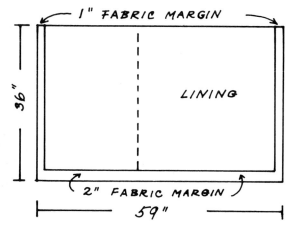

2. Unfold and cut lining in the same manner. The first piece will measure 34 by 45 inches; the second, 12 by 34 inches. Pin and sew the two 34-inch edges together with a ½-inch seam allowance. Press seams open. The lining now measures 57 by 34 inches.

3. Place lining on top of fabric, right sides facing, leaving 1-inch margins of fabric on both sides and a 2-inch margin at the bottom. (See *Diagram 3-O2*.) Pin the seam lining to fabric on right and left sides, leaving a ½-inch seam allowance. Leave the bottom 2 inches of lining unsewn, to be hemmed later. Turn right side out; press seam; press lining and skirt bottom in accordance with seam.

4. Topstitch skirt lining together, ⅛ inch in from top edges. Mark and pin darts across lining of skirt, exactly as shown in *Diagram 3-O3*. Small darts measure 1 inch across and 3½ inches deep. Large darts are 2 inches across and 7 inches deep. Machine-stitch all darts through both thicknesses. Knot end-threads together and trim them. Press darts flat.

5. From remaining skirt fabric make waistband by cutting 2 strips, 1 measuring 2 by 36 inches, the other, 2 by 22½ inches. (See *Diagram 3-O4*.) Leaving a ¼-inch seam allowance, seam short ends together to make a long strip, 2 by 58 inches. Set aside.

6. From the same skirt fabric, cut a strip measuring 1¾ by 19 inches for the bow. (See *Diagram 3-O4*.) With right sides facing, fold strip

indicated by shaded area should be set aside for later use. Pin the newly cut 36-inch raw edge of the second piece to the 36-inch selvage of the first piece. Seam together, leaving a ½-inch seam allowance. Press seams open. You now have a piece measuring 59 by 36 inches.

DIAGRAM 3-O3

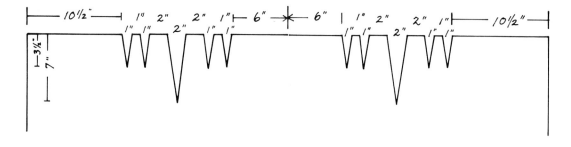

DIAGRAM 3-04

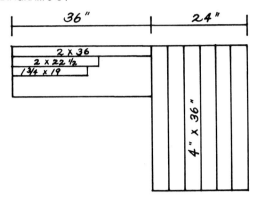

12. Press lining under ¼ inch. Pin to desired length and machine-stitch along edge. Sew double sets of hooks and eyes where indicated in *Diagram 3-05*. Sew bow to waistband. Wear skirt with ruffle going down left side.

DIAGRAM 3-05

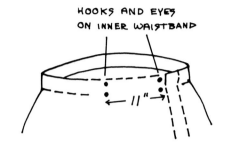

in half lengthwise and pin together. Stitch 1 short end to the long, raw edge, ¼ inch in from edge. Turn right side out; press flat; sew short, raw end under ¼ inch. Tie into bow and set aside.

7. Cut the last of the skirt fabric into 6 strips, each measuring 4 by 36 inches. (See *Diagram 3-04.*) Sew ¼-inch seams at short ends to make 1 continuous strip. Press seams open. Fold strip in half lengthwise, wrong sides facing; press flat. Gather along raw edge to make an even length of ruffle.

8. Hold skirt waistline to your own; determine where the hemline should be and mark it with a pin. Lay skirt out flat, and add ¼ inch to pinned hemline. Mark a straight line across length of skirt and cut along it.

9. Lay skirt out flat. Beginning at top right corner, pin raw edge of ruffle along right edge of skirt. Pin ruffle down right wrap side and all along bottom edge. Machine-stitch ¼ inch in from edges. Press seams toward inside of skirt.

10. Press short ends of waistband strip under ½ inch. Right sides facing, pin waistband edge to top edge of skirt, beginning at top right corner. Stitch together ¼ inch in from edge. Press flat. Press unsewn waistband edge under ¼ inch and machine-stitch. Fold waistband in half, lengthwise; press; pin inside edge in place; and sew, using a small hem-stitch.

11. Cut elastic to waist measurement. Run it through waistband casing, and secure it with stitches at both ends.

4
Sportswear and Casual Apparel

Dirty-Hands Smock

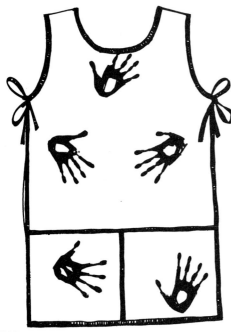

DIAGRAM 4-AA

This smock was designed by my friend Vivian Abell, with the help of one of her students, for the two of us to wear on our syndicated television craft show. It's a stylish solution to the problem of "Oh, dear! what if someone rings the doorbell while I'm doing this messy housework—or crafts project!"

MATERIALS

brown wrapping paper, equivalent in size to 4 sheets newspaper

2⅓ yards cotton or synthetic fabric, 36 inches wide, in solid color

1 package cotton seam binding, ½ inch wide, in contrasting color

1 yard grosgrain ribbon, ½ inch wide, to match seam binding

thread to match seam binding

1 small jar acrylic paint, to match seam binding

1. Enlarge smock and pocket pattern on brown wrapping paper. (See *Diagram 4-A1.*) Cut out.

2. If fabric as you bought it is folded lengthwise, unfold it. Fold fabric crosswise, bringing cut ends together. Pin paper pattern on fabric, and cut through both layers of fabric to make 2 pieces. Next, cut out pocket.

3. Place smock pieces with right sides facing, and seam shoulders together ½ inch from edge. Press shoulder seams open.

DIAGRAM 4-A1

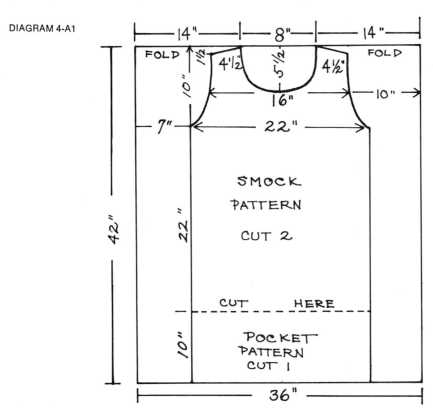

4. Turn bottom hem of the smock under ¼ inch and press. Stitch in place by hand or machine.

5. Turn pocket under ¼ inch all around. Press on fold. Fold entire package of seam binding in half lengthwise so that it is ¼ inch wide; press. Slip over pocket edges sandwich-style and pin. Sew around the edges and down the center of the pocket as shown in *Diagram 4-A2.*

DIAGRAM 4-A2

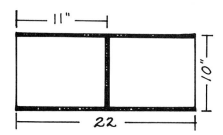

6. Bind the neckline and all around the edges of the smock by folding seam binding over raw edges and stitching in place.

7. Sew pocket to the bottom of the apron as shown in *Diagram 4-AA.*

8. Cut grosgrain ribbon into four 9-inch lengths. Sew ribbons just below each armhole on the front and back to form the side ties of the smock.

9. Cover a table or the floor with newspaper, and lay smock out flat. (Do not double the fabric when printing in the following step, or the paint may soak through from 1 side to the other.)

10. Coat your hand with acrylic paint and press on smock wherever desired. Allow handprints to overlap the pocket to tie it in to the smock design. After printing, wash paint off hands with soap and water. Let smock dry flat.

Beaded Slippers

DIAGRAM 4-BB

Dime-store terry cloth scuffs become pretty enough for a gift, while you put a lazy summer afternoon to good use.

MATERIALS

1 thin or beading needle
polyester thread to match scuffs
1 pair dime-store terry cloth scuffs
1 tube or 2 strands beads, size 11°, in green plus 1 other color
2 small pearls, about ¼-inch diameter
½ to ¾ yard velvet ribbon, ¼ inch wide, in contrasting color
white resin glue

1. Thread beading needle with a 20-inch length of thread, and knot the end of the thread. Insert needle up through the center of the scuff instep, from the inside to the outside. Put 9 colored (not green) beads on the needle, slide them down onto the thread, and position them as shown for center row of beads on a petal in *Diagram 4-B1.* Push needle through to wrong side of scuff instep, and bring needle up again at base of petal. Put 7 beads on needle for each of the side rows of the petals. Follow numbers in *Diagram 4-B1* for needle, going up at 1, 3, and 5 and down at 2, 4, and 6. Tack in place securely. Flower has 8 petals in all, as shown.

2. Tack approximately ½ inch of green beads

DIAGRAM 4-B1

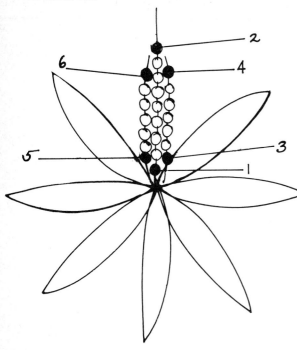

in place to form first part of stem, following *Diagram 4-B2.*

3. Make a leaf on either side at the base of this stem, using ½ inch of green beads.

4. Continue stem with 1 inch of green beads, as shown in *Diagram 4-B2.*

5. Make tiny leaves on either side of the base of this stem, using ¼ inch of green beads.

6. Make a blossom of colored (not green) beads, using a center row of 7 beads and 2 side rows of 5 beads.

7. Repeat stem, leaves, and blossom design on opposite side of flower.

8. Repeat beading design in steps 2 to 7 on the other slipper.

9. Sew one ¼-inch pearl to the center of each flower (not to the blossom) on the slippers.

10. Cut the velvet ribbon to fit the edges of the toe and instep openings on each slipper. Glue in place, and let dry completely.

11. To wash, dip by hand into sudsy water, rinse, and dry in a warm place other than a clothes dryer.

Holiday variation: Work flowers in red beads, trim slippers with red or green ribbon, and tuck them under the Christmas tree for someone you love.

DIAGRAM 4-B2

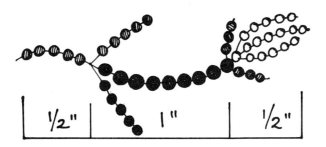

Crochet-look Fall Ensemble

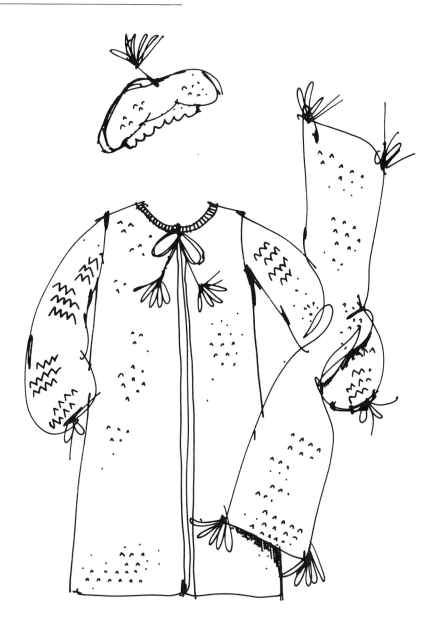

DIAGRAM 4-CC

I'm always a little envious of my friends who knit their own coats and sweaters. I can do it, but I just don't have the time. So I have devised this easy way to make a little hand knitting look like much more. The secret is to use the machine-made knit- and crochet-look fabrics now available; *some of them are really fabulous and look like the real thing. Best of all, they're not expensive. If you can't knit, or don't want to, make the coat sleeveless and bind the armholes with fold-over braid to wear as a long tunic.*

MATERIALS

2½ to 3 yards synthetic knit- or crochet-look fabric (2½ yards are sufficient for up to misses size 14), at least 45 inches wide, in solid color

thread to match fabric

2 skeins Orlon acrylic knitting worsted, 3½ or 4 ounces each, in variegated colors to complement fabric

1 yarn needle

chalk

1 piece of string, about 12 inches long

2 packages rayon seam binding, to match fabric

22 inches (approximately) elastic (exact length determined by your head measurement), ½ inch wide

3 to 3½ yards fold-over cotton or Orlon braid, ½ inch wide, to match fabric

1 pair knitting needles, size #19 or junior jumbo 14 inches long

1. *Scarf:* Unfold the fabric and lay it in front of you so that the 2½-yard length runs from top to bottom. Cut off a piece the full width of the fabric and 21 inches long. Set the remaining fabric aside. (See *Diagram 4-C1.*)

DIAGRAM 4-C1

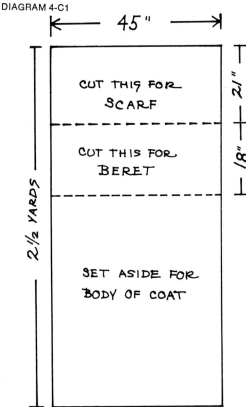

2. Fold cut fabric in half lengthwise, with right sides together, so that it forms a double piece 10½ inches wide. Pin along the 3 open edges to hold in place. Machine-stitch the long pinned side and 1 short side, ½ inch from edge, removing pins as you sew. (See *Diagram 4-C2.*)

DIAGRAM 4-C2

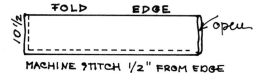

3. Turn scarf right side out and press with a steam iron, using a pressing cloth.

4. Turn open edge under ½ inch on both sides and press in place. Sew opening closed with tiny overcasting stitches.

5. Using knitting worsted, make 8 tassels, each 3½ inches long, winding yarn about 35 times for each tassel. Do not trim away extra yarn that secures the top of the tassel.

6. Each short end of the scarf will have 4 tassels. To fasten tassels to scarf, thread yarn needle with length of yarn attached to the top of 1 tassel, and insert needle in fabric at 1 corner of the scarf about ½ inch in from the edges. Knot yarn to secure, and cut off excess. Attach remaining tassels so that they are evenly spaced in the same way.

7. *Beret:* With fabric in the same position as it was for the scarf, cut off a piece the full width of the fabric and 18 inches long. (See *Diagram 4-C1.*) Set the remaining fabric aside.

8. Lay this 18-inch-deep piece of fabric out flat. With chalk and string, draw 2 circles on it, each 17 inches in diameter.

9. Cut out circles, handling fabric carefully to avoid raveling.

10. Place circles together with wrong sides facing. Pin around the edges and machine-stitch completely around, ¼ inch in from the edge. Remove pins as you go.

11. Pin so that seam binding edge just covers stitching on circles, and machine-stitch seam binding in place. Stitches should lie exactly over previous row of stitches.

12. Fold seam binding over row of stitches to the inside of the circle to form casing. Fabric will show ¼ inch beyond the folded outer edge of the seam binding. Press seam binding in place with a steam iron. (See *Diagram 4-C3*.)

DIAGRAM 4-C3

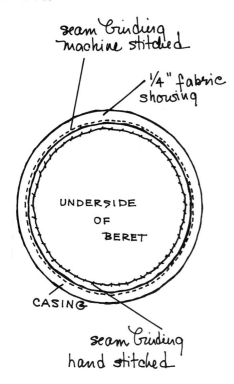

13. Taking tiny stitches by hand, sew the open edge of the seam binding to inside of the beret, stitching through only the top layer of fabric as it faces you. Leave a ½-inch opening for inserting the elastic.

14. Run elastic through casing, adjust to head size, and take a few stitches to secure it. Sew opening closed.

15. Cut three 18-inch lengths of knitting worsted and tie together 4 inches in from one end. Braid worsted until there is a 4-inch length. Tie a knot to secure the braiding, leaving 4 inches of loose yarn after the knot.

16. Make a 3½-inch tassel, winding the yarn 100 times so that the tassel is very full.

17. Thread yarn needle with the three 4-inch ends of yarn at 1 end of braid, and insert it through the open weave of the fabric at the exact top center of the beret. Remove needle and tie strands around fabric to secure. Cut off excess yarn on the inside of the beret, leaving ends about 1 inch long. Tie the other 4-inch loose strands of the braided section through the top of the tassel, knot very securely, and cut off excess yarn close to knot.

18. *Coat:* To determine the width of the coat, measure your hips at the widest part and add 3 inches. (For example, if your hips measure 38 inches, add 3 inches and you will get a total of 41 inches needed for the width of the coat.)

19. Lay remaining fabric out lengthwise and flat, with the wrong side facing up. Measure from the left selvage for half of your total in step 1 (20½ inches in the example) and mark with a pin.

20. Bring the left selvage over to the point where the pin is. (See *Diagram 4-C4*.) This point marks ½ the desired width of the coat at the hips.

DIAGRAM 4-C4

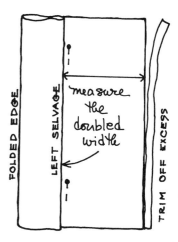

You now have the fabric doubled on the left side measuring ¼ of the total measurement in step 1 (10¼ inches in our example). Now from this pin, measure off another half of the step-1 measurement (20½ inches in example) and cut fabric evenly from bottom to top. Set remaining fabric (if you have any) aside for another project.

21. Carefully fold this cut edge on your right to the left, doubling it up to meet the pin and having it even with the other side. Handle this raw edge carefully to avoid raveling. Remove the pin you used as a marker; pin doubled fabric together at top in several places for the next step.

22. Cut out the neck opening and armholes following *Diagram 4-C5.* Remove all pins.

DIAGRAM 4-C5

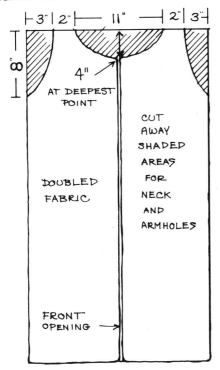

23. Stay-stitch, by machine, ⅛ inch in from the edge, along all raw edges, including the hem of the coat, the front, the neckline, the armholes, and the shoulders. For very loose knits, add a second row of machine stay-stitching ⅛ inch from the first one, to further secure the edges. With right sides facing, sew shoulder seams ½ inch from edge. Press seams open.

24. Starting at the bottom of 1 front edge, pin the fold-over braid up along the front, around the neckline, and down the other front. Machine-stitch braid in place, removing pins as you go.

25. Machine-stitch seam binding to the bot-

tom hem edge of the coat. Do not turn up the hem yet. Set the coat aside for now.

26. *Coat sleeves:* With knitting needles, cast on 40 stitches. Work in stockinette stitch (knit 1 row, purl 1 row) for 45 rows. Bind off loosely, leaving 1 yard of yarn. Repeat to make the second sleeve.

27. Thread a yarn needle with the yarn attached to 1 sleeve, and sew up the sleeve seam to form a tube. Repeat on the other sleeve.

28. Pin the bound-off edges of 1 sleeve to 1 armhole of the coat. Use yarn to sew the sleeve in place, having the sleeve overlapping the outside of the armhole of the coat by ½ inch and keeping the sleeve seam at the inside of the coat side. Repeat with the other sleeve.

29. Cut six 18-inch lengths of yarn. Knot 3 of these pieces together 2 inches in from the ends, and braid them until there are 2 inches of yarn left; knot. Repeat with the other 3 pieces of yarn to make a second braid.

30. Sew 1 braided piece to each side of the top front opening for ties.

31. Make 2 tassels the same size as the ones you made in step 5 of the scarf. Tie 1 tassel to each loose end of the neck ties in the same way you attached the large tassel to the top of the beret (step 17, above).

32. Cut 6 more 18-inch lengths of knitting worsted; divide into 2 groups of 3 strands. For each group, knot 2 inches in from the end and braid until 2 inches from the other end to complete 2 more braids.

33. Attach a small safety pin to 1 knot of 1 braid and weave through the stitches of the second knitted row from the bottom of the sleeve edge. Adjust to wrist size and tie braid ends in a bow. Repeat with other braid on other sleeve. Cut the ends of the braids so that 1 inch of yarn remains. (There are no tassels on these sleeve ties.)

34. *Coat hem:* Try on coat and turn up hemline to the desired length. Press hem in place, using a steam iron and pressing cloth. Hand-stitch hem.

35. Press the entire outfit to block it before wearing. Store the coat as you would a sweater, folding it and laying it flat. Do not hang the coat on a hanger or it might stretch.

Lace-and-Denim Patio Ensemble

MATERIALS

1 man's blue workshirt, small size
8 round pearl buttons, ⅜-inch or ½-inch diameter
8 yards (approximately) preruffled nylon or cotton eyelet edging, ¾ inch wide, in white
3 commercial monogram letters in your initials, 2 inches high, in white
1 pair blue jeans
1 blue denim beach hat or white sailor's hat
white resin glue

DIAGRAM 4-DD

Transform work clothes into an outfit for a patio party or any other festive and informal occasion. This outfit will cost only about $12, even if you use top-quality blue jeans (which I heartily recommend).

1. *Shirt:* Cut shirt buttons off the front placket and cuffs, and pick out remaining threads. Replace with pearl buttons.

2. Cut 2 short strips of nylon or eyelet edging to fit across the top of the shirt pockets plus ½ inch. Pin strips across tops of pockets, turning ends under ¼ inch, and sew in place.

3. Cut a short strip of nylon or eyelet edging to fit around the collar plus ½ inch. Pin on collar, turning under ¼ inch at ends, and sew in place.

4. Cut 4 short strips of nylon or eyelet edging to fit around the cuffs plus ½ inch. Pin 1 each around bottom and top edges of each cuff, turning ends under ¼ inch, and sew.

5. Lay shirt flat. Cut 1 strip of edging to fit the length of the right side of the placket (as you look at it) plus ½ inch. Pin in place just behind the front edge of the placket, turning ends under ¼ inch, and sew.

6. Saving 2 yards of edging for the blue jeans, pin the remaining edging just behind the left edge of the placket and all around the bottom edge of the shirt; sew. Wear shirt out, as an overblouse.

7. By hand, stitch monogram letters across the left pocket, arranging letters diagonally.

8. *Blue jeans:* Wash blue jeans before trimming with edging, to remove excess dye. Dry them and iron well. (When washing blue jeans, by hand or machine, always use cool water so that they will not "bleed" onto the edging.)

9. Cut nylon or eyelet edging in 6 strips long enough to fit around the width of the pants leg plus ½ inch. For the first row of edging, pin 1 strip around the very bottom of 1 pants leg, turning under ¼ inch at ends, and sew.

10. Repeat for a second and third row up the leg, leaving 1 inch between each row of edging. Repeat on other leg.

11. *Hat:* Cut 1 strip of edging to fit the seam where crown of hat meets the brim plus ½ inch. Cut another strip to fit the edge of the brim plus ½ inch.

12. Glue the edging strips in their appropriate places, turning under ¼ inch at ends. Let dry.

Terry Towel Beach Shift

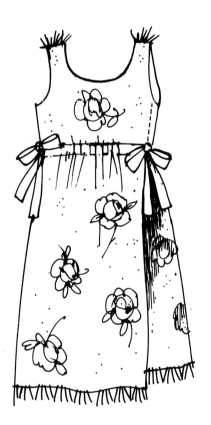

DIAGRAM 4-EE

I'm sure I'm not the only one who often has to do some marketing after leaving the beach or the swimming club. Any beach robe I put on over my wet bathing suit invariably gets wet when I ride in

the car. To avoid this, I have designed this open-sided shift; the back flap can be slipped over the back of your seat while you sit on a towel to absorb the excess water from your bathing suit. You'll be presentable when you get to the supermarket, dry when you get home, and the car seat won't be ruined.

MATERIALS

2 matching terry cloth bath towels, preferably fringed, 24 inches wide
bonding net
thread to match towels
1 package wide cotton seam binding, to match towels
2 yards grosgrain ribbon, ¾ inch wide, in any desired color

1. Cut armholes and neck opening from each towel, following *Diagram 4-E1.*

DIAGRAM 4-E1

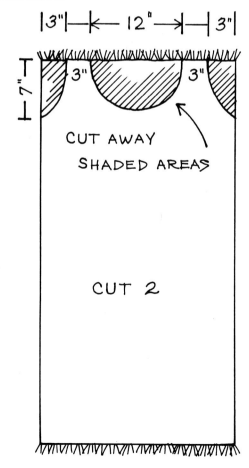

2. Place towels together with wrong sides facing, matching up armholes, and seam together (or bond with bonding net) at the shoulders, directly below the fringe, so that fringe lies freely. Overlap side seams ½ inch below armholes and seam or bond for 4 inches as shown in *Diagram 4-E2.*

DIAGRAM 4-E2

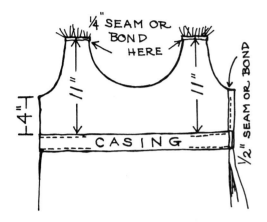

3. To finish neck opening and armholes, turn under ¼ inch and sew; or finish by bonding, turning raw edges under ½ inch all around and using ½-inch-wide strips of bonding net.

4. Using wide seam binding, pin and stitch a casing to both front and back, as shown in *Diagram 4-E2,* 11 inches down from the top of the shoulder, or length you need to come below bust in front. Sew casing; do not bond it or there will be no space through which to insert the ribbon.

5. Cut grosgrain ribbon into 1-yard lengths, and pull 1 strip each through the front and back casings.

6. Tie ribbons at each side of the shift when wearing.

Poolside Miniskirt

DIAGRAM 4-FF

Here's another after-swim fashion that's absorbent and cool, made out of two terry cloth aprons. I wear it with a midriff top. The directions below will fit dress sizes 10 to 14.

MATERIALS

2 matching terry cloth aprons, with gathered skirts
¼ yard bonding net
2 snaps or 2 hooks and eyes
thread to match aprons

1. Cut bonding net into 2 strips, each measuring 2 inches wide and as long as the apron side seams. Place aprons together with wrong sides facing, and lay flat. Cut the 2 ties off the top front apron, leaving ¼ inch free. Turn the ends under and secure with either bonding net or needle and thread.

2. Overlap the right side of the back apron over the right side of the front apron. Both apron sides overlap both front apron sides. Pin in place. Try on skirt and adjust pins and depth of the overlap to your size. (See *Diagram 4-F1.*) Sandwich bonding net between the overlapping sides, re-

moving pins as you go, and bond together, following package directions.

3. Repeat for the left side of the skirt, leaving an 8-inch opening below the waistband. Cut off the extra 8 inches of bonding net and set aside for another use. (See *Diagram 4-F1.*)

DIAGRAM 4-F1

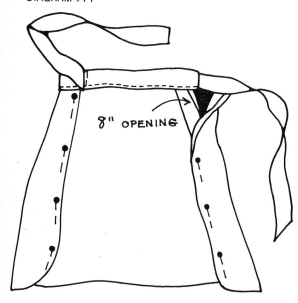

4. Sew 1 snap or 1 hook and eye at waistband on left side and another halfway down side opening.

5. To wear, fasten closures and tie a bow at center front of skirt.

Knit-Shirt Midriff Top

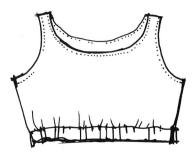

DIAGRAM 4-GG

Nothing is more annoying than to purchase a pretty knit shirt only to find that after a few washings, the bottom has become too baggy to wear. For a knit shirt like this or for any favorite shirt that could use a new look, a quick solution is to convert it to a midriff top. Although a cotton blouse does not get baggy at the bottom, you may want to give a new look to a blouse by following the same directions.

MATERIALS

1 cotton knit shirt (a sleeveless one is best)
polyester thread in matching color
elastic (length determined by rib cage measurement plus 1 inch), ½ inch wide

1. Cut off the knit shirt 2 inches below lowest part of bust.

2. Turn under the raw edge of the shirt ¼ inch and press flat. Machine- or hand-stitch into place.

3. Turn this same edge up ¾ inch more and press flat. Again, stitch in place, to form a casing for the elastic.

4. Insert the elastic into the casing and secure it with a few stitches.

Hostess Gown

DIAGRAM 4-HH

A striking hostess gown, which can be made in a few hours and costs a fraction of what you'd pay for it in a boutique, starts with a cotton knit shirt and a length of pretty fabric. A variation made with a blouse is included. For a gown with a pleated skirt, use prepleated fabric.

MATERIALS

1 good-quality cotton knit pullover shirt, in your size, in a solid color

cotton fabric (45-inch length by desired width of hip plus 10 inches; about 45 inches is right for dress sizes 12 to 14, so that, roughly, you will have a 45- by 45-inch square), in coordinated color or pattern

thread to match predominant color

no-roll elastic (length determined by waist measurement plus 1 inch), ½ inch wide

1. Try on knit shirt and mark with pin where your natural waistline falls. Measure and mark evenly 1½ inches below the natural waistline and cut off the bottom of the shirt.

2. Fold skirt fabric with right sides together along the length or selvage. This is the back seam of the gown skirt. Sew the seam and press open.

3. Gather the top edge of the skirt and adjust it to fit the bottom edge of the knit shirt. Edges will be joined together just below your natural waistline, since this design has a slightly blousy effect.

4. Hold shirt upside down, with right side facing out, and slip top of skirt, also with right side facing out, inside of shirt. The bottom of the knit shirt should extend about 1 inch over the skirt top. Ease the gathers around and pin. Try on garment and adjust to fit.

5. Fold under raw edge of shirt top ⅛ inch; pin. Now topstitch the skirt to the shirt along folded edge. Then topstitch a second row directly above and exactly ⅝ inch from first row of stitching. This will form a casing through

DIAGRAM 4-H1

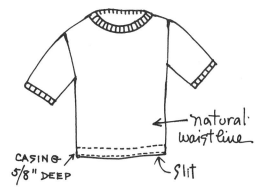

natural waistline

CASING ⅝" DEEP

slit

which to put the elastic. Make a tiny slit on the inside of 1 side of the casing to insert the elastic through. (See *Diagram 4-H1.*)

6. Insert elastic through casing and secure the ends of the elastic together by machine or hand stitching.

7. Turn the hem of the skirt under ¼ inch and press it in place. Turn it up again 4 or 5 inches to desired hemline. Try on to check length, press in place, and hand-stitch hem.

Variation: A variation on this same pattern can be made using a blouse that buttons down the front. Cut and join the bottom edge of the blouse to the fabric skirt in the same manner as the shirt, but position the skirt seam in front to line up with the blouse opening. Button the lowest button on the blouse before pinning the gathered skirt to the blouse. Use a grosgrain ribbon, 1½ to 2 yards long, through the casing instead of elastic, and tie in front in a soft bow with streamers, to cover the front seam of the skirt.

Embroidery-trimmed Sweater

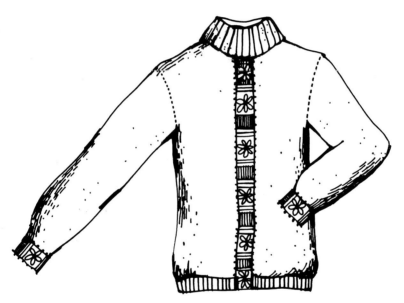

DIAGRAM 4-II

Try this easy and dramatic face lift for a plain sweater that you've grown tired of.

MATERIALS

1¼ yards embroidered cotton ribbon, 2 inches wide, in contrasting color to turtleneck
1 ladies' turtleneck sweater with long sleeves, in solid color
white resin glue
thread to match sweater
4 snaps

1. Cut ribbon long enough to reach from the base of the turtleneck to the bottom of the sweater, plus an extra 3 or 4 inches.

2. In the exact center front of the sweater, pin the ribbon vertically from the neck to the bottom, turning ribbon edges under ¼ inch at top and placing the top edge of the ribbon under the turtleneck. Stretch sweater slightly as you pin—but not too much or the ribbon will look puckered. Glue ribbon securely, removing pins as you work. At the bottom edge, turn the ribbon under ½ inch

and glue to secure. Cut off any excess. Let dry completely.

3. To make embroidered cuffs, cut 2 pieces of ribbon to the length of the wrist measurement plus 1 inch. Turn both ends of each of these pieces under ¼ inch and glue to secure. Let dry.

4. By hand, tack 1 short edge of 1 ribbon piece to the sleeve seam on the outside of the sweater cuff. (See *Diagram 4-I1.*) Sew 2 snaps

DIAGRAM 4-I1

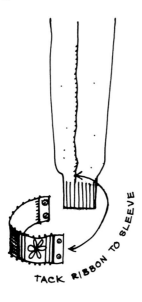

TACK RIBBON TO SLEEVE

to this edge of the ribbon. Sew other snap parts in corresponding position on the other side of the ribbon, which hangs free, so that when ribbon cuff is snapped in place, it will fit snugly around the wrist.

5. Finish the other cuff in the same way.

6. Should sweater become soiled, dry clean.

Rejuvenated Jumper

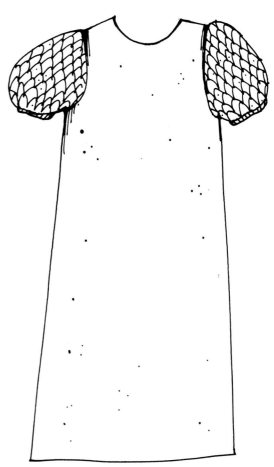

DIAGRAM 4-JJ

If you have a jumper that you've worn so much you hate to even look at it, why not convert it to a dress? Give it a new look by adding hand-knit sleeves in matching or contrasting colors. With the aid of jumbo needles, the transformation can be quickly accomplished. If you prefer not to knit, use ready-made knit fabric or, thriftier still, cut out the sleeves from an old sweater and attach them to the jumper. The neck of the sweater, if it is still in good shape, can be converted to a dickey to set into the jumper neckline or to wear under a blazer.

MATERIALS

1 jumper

2 skeins 4-ply knitting worsted, 2 ounces each, in 2 different colors

1 pair knitting needles, size #35

thread to match jumper

1. Working with 2 strands of yarn together throughout, cast on 25 stitches. Work in ribbing (knit 1, purl 1) for 16 rows. Bind off very loosely, leaving about 24 inches of loose yarn.

2. Sew the inner arm seam together to form a cylinder.

3. Repeat steps 1 and 2 to make the other sleeve.

4. Pin 1 end of 1 sleeve evenly inside the edge of 1 armhole of the jumper; sew in by hand, removing pins as you go. Set in other sleeve in the same way.

Sporty Suede-Cloth Jerkin

DIAGRAM 4-KK

This jerkin is sure to liven up the wardrobe of any woman you know. It will lend special charm to a turtleneck sweater and pants outfit.

MATERIALS

brown wrapping paper, equivalent in size to 2 sheets newspaper

1 yard suede cloth, 48 to 50 inches wide

thread to match fabric

3 yards (approximately) embroidered ribbon, 2 inches wide, in coordinating color

white resin glue

8 inches nylon fastening tape

1. Following *Diagram 4-K1,* cut out a paper pattern for the jerkin. Note that width equals ½ the bust measurement plus 3 inches.

2. Fold fabric in half crosswise, and pin pattern on, placing shoulders at fold. Cut out. Unpin pattern.

DIAGRAM 4-K1

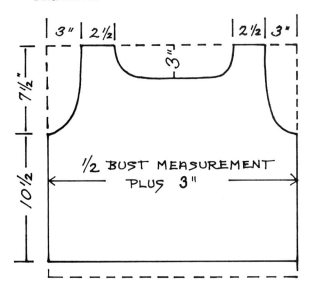

3. To fit bustline, slip jerkin over shoulders and, looking in a mirror, put a straight pin into fabric at the fullest point on each side of the bust. Remove jerkin and lay it out flat on the table.

4. Mark a line from each straight pin to the front bottom corners of jerkin. Fold and pin a dart down each side, tapering from nothing at bust point to ½ inch at bottom corners. (See *Diagram 4-K2*.) Stitch darts in place, using sewing machine. (Sew suede cloth with medium-sized needle.)

DIAGRAM 4-K2

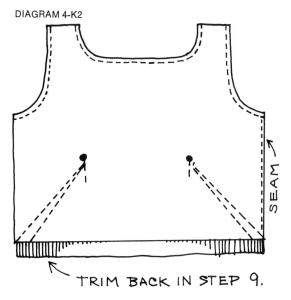

TRIM BACK IN STEP 9.

5. Turn jerkin inside out and pin the front to the back on the wrong sides. Since the back of the jerkin hangs lower than the front because of the darts, be sure to line sides up evenly at the armholes; bottom will be trimmed later. (See *Diagram 4-K2*.) Sew side seam on the right ½ inch from edge.

6. Turn jerkin right side out. Fold raw edges of neck and armholes under ¼ inch and machine topstitch in place close to the edge. Put a second row of topstitching ⅛ inch in from this first row.

7. Cut embroidered ribbon into 10 equal lengths, each at least 11 inches long. If the ribbon has a repeat pattern, allow enough ribbon so that the design falls in the same place on each strip.

8. Turn 1 raw bottom end of each ribbon piece under ¼ inch and glue in place. Let dry completely.

9. Trim off the excess fabric at the bottom back of the jerkin so that it is even with the front. Turn under the bottom edge of jerkin on both front

DIAGRAM 4-K3

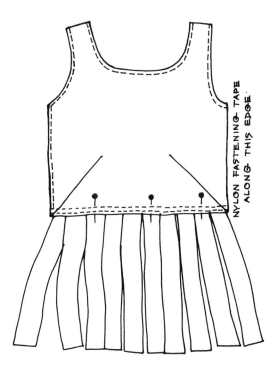

82

and back for ½ inch and sew in place with 2 rows of topstitching placed ¼ inch apart.

10. Turn left side edges under ¼ inch and topstitch in place.

11. Pin the 10, raw, unglued, ribbon ends behind the front bottom edges of the jerkin with the edges touching or evenly spaced, depending on width of ribbons and jerkin. (See *Diagram 4-K3.*) Machine-stitch ribbons in place, ⅛ to ¼ inch up from previous topstitching. Make sure all ribbons are sewn securely with this topstitching.

12. Sew nylon fastening tape to the underside of the left front and to the outside of the left back. Front laps over back.

Pillowcase Nightgown

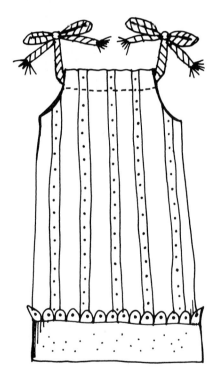

DIAGRAM 4-LL

When you buy pillowcases in packages of two, make this breezy nightgown from one case and use the second one on your bed. This design is nearly effortless to make because it involves no

sewing. It is most effective in a pretty print or pastel fabric, scalloped or embroidered on the edge. A standard pillowcase will fit girls and women up to a misses size 14, or up to a size 38 hip.

MATERIALS

1 standard pillowcase, in any desired color or pattern
1 package bonding net
2½ yards upholstery cording, ¼- or ½-inch diameter

1. Carefully open the top seam of the pillowcase, using a thread clipper, a pair of tiny scissors, or a straight pin. Now open both side seams 2 inches down from the top in the same manner. Remove threads and press out the seams.

2. With pillowcase right side out, turn raw edges of both front and back down 2 inches from the top; press. These will be bonded in place in step 5; pressing will hold them in place until then.

3. Cut out armholes 3½ inches in from the side and 8 inches down and clip along the curve, as shown in *Diagram 4-L1.*

DIAGRAM 4-L1

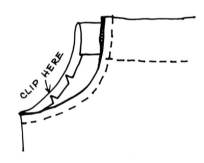

4. Cut bonding net in strips ¾ inch wide to fit the edges of the armholes. Turn under raw edges of armholes ¾ inch and bond in place.

5. Turn pillowcase inside out. Cut 2 strips of bonding net ½ inch wide and long enough to go across the top edge of the nightgown. Secure raw top edges with bonding net strips, leaving 1½ inches open for casing as shown in *Diagram 4-L2.* Turn right side out.

6. Cut upholstery cording into two 1¼-yard lengths, and insert 1 strip in back and 1 in front casing.

7. Knot each of the 4 ends of the cording about 1½ inches in from the end, and fray for a tassel effect.

8. To wear, tie front to back at shoulders.

DIAGRAM 4-L2

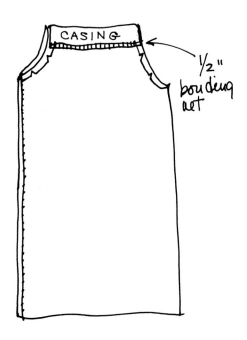

Pearl-trimmed Lounging Slippers

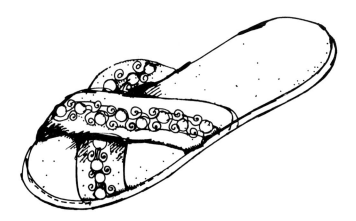

DIAGRAM 4-MM

A pair of dime-store terry scuffs get a boutique look in less than an hour and for very little money *—a perk-up for you or a perfect gift for a friend or relative.*

MATERIALS

1 yard gimp upholstery braid, to match or contrast
   with scuffs
1 pair terry cloth sandal-type scuffs, with crisscross
   straps
white resin glue
white thread
50 (approximately) pearls, ¼-inch diameter

1. Cut a piece of gimp upholstery braid to fit each crisscross strip of instep, allowing 1 extra inch on each (4 pieces of gimp in all).

2. Glue a gimp strip to the center of each crisscross strip, stretching the crisscross part slightly as you work to allow for "give" when wearing. Tuck ends of braid in as close as possible to the sole of the slipper and glue down remainder of gimp. Let dry completely.

3. With needle and white thread, tack a pearl at ½-inch intervals across the length of each piece of braid. Start and finish each strip by taking several small stitches in place to secure.

Patchwork-on-Patchwork Tunic

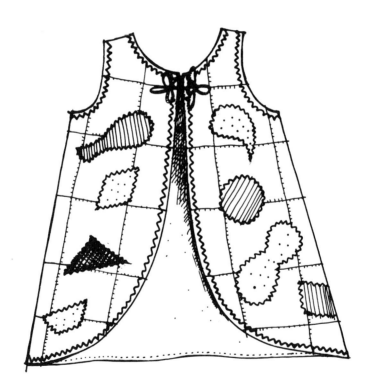

DIAGRAM 4-NN

I thought of calling this project the "End of the Book Tunic" because it is constructed entirely of felt scraps left over after I had completed all the *other projects. Then I decided that this design really belonged right here. Of course, you don't have to wait until you make everything else to make this tunic. Just gather up the scraps you have on hand, buy whatever else you need, and get started. See Chapter 2 if you want to make your own frog for the closing.*

MATERIALS

1 commercial pattern for open-front hip-length tunic
felt for lining (amount indicated on pattern for 72-inch fabric), in any desired color
felt scraps to make equal amount of patchwork fabric, or fifteen to twenty 9- by 12-inch felt rectangles, in assorted bright colors
thread to match felt lining
2 packages wide rickrack, to match felt lining
1 frog, 1½ to 3 inches, in contrasting color to felt lining, or 1 yard cording, ¼ inch wide (if you make your own frog)
pinking shears

1. Cut out felt lining according to pattern directions and construct, omitting facings but making darts if the pattern calls for them.

2. Cut felt scraps or rectangles into small rectangles of various dimensions, from 2 to 5 inches. Assemble as described in Patchwork method 1, Chapter 2, until you have 3 pieces the sizes of the pattern pieces for back, left front, and right front. Lay out pattern on felt patchwork fabric and cut out the tunic pieces. Construct, following pattern directions and omitting facings. Press seams open as you go.

3. Insert lining into tunic with wrong sides facing, and pin together at neckline armholes, front opening, and hem.

4. Topstitch lining to patchwork tunic ⅛ inch from edge, removing the pins as you go.

5. Machine-stitch rickrack around armholes, neck, front opening, and hemline of tunic just over the topstitching.

6. Sew frog to the top of the front opening at the neckline on both sides.

7. You may complete the tunic and leave it as is in step 6. Or you may cut odd-shaped pieces of 3 or 4 different colors from felt, using pinking shears, and glue to the front and back of the tunic at random. Overlap each irregular piece over the joining of several squares; do not center them within a square.

5
Belts, Jewelry, and Other Ornaments

Macramé Evening Belt

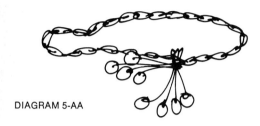

DIAGRAM 5-AA

Macramé is fun to do, and it's even more fun when you use an unexpected material such as gold cord gift tie. Make this evening belt to just fit your waist or loose enough to sit low on your hips. Either way, you can't possibly spend more than $2 on the materials for it. If you are not already familiar with the square knot, see the instructions and diagrams for macramé in Chapter 2. It is equally at home worn with a short wool dress or a long brocade gown.

MATERIALS

2 spools gift tie cord, each 25 feet, in gold
macramé board
T-pins
8 paillettes, in gold

1. Unwind gold cord from 1 spool, fold, and cut it exactly in half. Repeat with the other spool of cord, to make 4 strands in all.

2. Knot each of the 8 ends of the 4 strands very close to the edge to prevent raveling.

3. Knot all 4 strands together 6 inches from the end.

4. Work on macramé board or other flat surface; use T-pins to secure knots as you work. Proceed to make square knots until the desired length is reached, or until you are about 6 inches from the ends. (For a hip-hugger belt, length of knotted section should equal waist measurement plus 6 inches.) Make knots as close together as possible; since gold cord is slippery, you can later pull knots farther apart if you so desire.

5. After the last row of square knots, cut off excess cord, leaving loose ends 6 inches long.

6. Cut off all old knots at both ends of belt.

7. Slip 1 paillette on the end of each strand and secure with a knot. Cut off any excess cord.

Felt Flower Cummerbund

DIAGRAM 5-BB

Please don't limit yourself to the flower-and-stem design when you make this felt cummerbund. Put your own design talent to work and use your initials, a map of your town or state, an animal motif, your zodiac sign, or whatever else you can come up with.

MATERIALS

⅓ yard felt, in any desired color
tracing paper
2 felt rectangles, 9 by 12 inches, in green and any
　　contrasting color
thread to match large felt piece
2 small cosmetic cotton balls
3 inches nylon fastening tape

1. Following *Diagram 5-B1,* cut 2 of the belt patterns from the ⅓ yard felt, to fit your waist measurement plus 1 inch extra on each end. Set aside.

DIAGRAM 5-B1

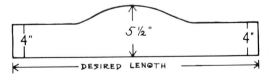

DIAGRAM 5-B2

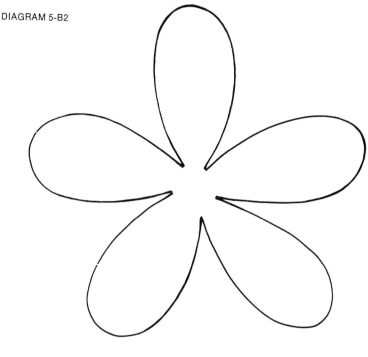

2. Trace or draw the flower shape from *Diagram 5-B2* on the contrasting color felt rectangle, and cut out.

3. Trace or draw the stem and the leaf shapes from *Diagram 5-B3* on the green felt, and cut out these pieces.

4. Position the stem and leaves on belt center as shown in project illustration; glue. Let dry.

5. Position the flower shape in the center of 1 belt piece. By hand, sew the edges of the petals to the belt piece, using tiny overcasting stitches.

6. Make a tiny slit in the center of the flower extending ¼ inch into each petal, as shown in *Diagram 5-B4*. (A pair of manicure scissors is good for this.) Using a pointed object, such as a pin or knitting needle, push about ⅓ of a cotton ball into each flower petal to give a raised effect.

7. From contrasting color felt, cut a strip measuring 2½ by 3 inches. Fold in half lengthwise, and make slits through the folded edge every ¼ inch all the way across, cutting from folded edge to within ¼ inch of the opposite (unfolded) edges. Glue these unfolded edges together. (See *Diagram 5-B5.*) Let dry completely.

DIAGRAM 5-B3

DIAGRAM 5-B4

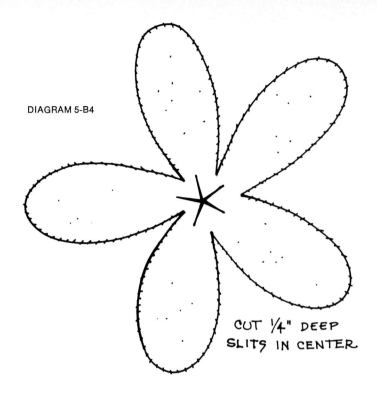

CUT ¼" DEEP
SLITS IN CENTER

DIAGRAM 5-B5

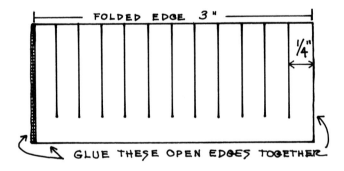

FOLDED EDGE 3"

¼"

GLUE THESE OPEN EDGES TOGETHER

8. Roll strip tightly from 1 short end to the other. Glue loose end to secure and let dry completely.

9. Press thumb down into slits, flattening them so that they resemble the ruffled center part of a flower. Glue in place at center of flower to conceal slits.

10. Glue front of the belt to the second belt piece (the back), or topstitch by hand or machine.

11. Cut nylon fastening tape in half and glue vertically to ends of the belt, placing 1 strip on the outer face of 1 end of the belt and 1 strip on the inner face of the opposite end. Overlap the nylon fastening tape strips to secure when wearing the belt.

Fancy Fish Belt

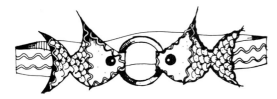

DIAGRAM 5-CC

Glittering sequin scales highlight the dramatic fish clasps on this festive belt. It's such a charming design that you'll undoubtedly want to make extras to give as gifts during the holiday season.

MATERIALS

1 sheet tracing paper
⅛ yard felt, in any desired color
white resin glue
1 package narrow rickrack, in gold
1 package paillettes, in assorted colors
1 brass drapery ring, 2-inch diameter
2 inches nylon fastening tape

1. Trace fish from *Diagram 5-C1* and cut out. Pin tracing paper pattern to felt and cut out. Repeat until you have 4 fish. Stack fish 2 together and glue to secure. Now you have 2 double-layered felt fish.

2. Glue rickrack completely around edges of both fish, positioning them so that they are facing each other. Glue around outside of the fish and around the gills, as shown in *Diagram 5-C1*.

DIAGRAM 5-C1

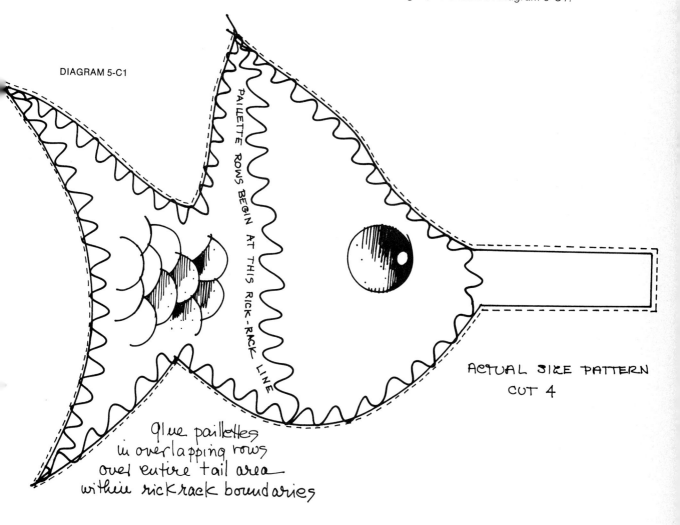

PAILLETTE ROWS BEGIN AT THIS RICK-RACK LINE

ACTUAL SIZE PATTERN
CUT 4

glue paillettes
in overlapping rows
over entire tail area
within rickrack boundaries

3. Glue paillettes in overlapping rows, beginning at the gills and working toward the tail of the fish. Use manicure scissors to cut paillettes wherever necessary to trim them to the shape of the fish.

4. Select 1 paillette for the eye of each fish, and glue it in place. Let dry completely.

5. The distance from the tail of 1 fish to the tail of the other fish including the curtain ring will measure about 9½ inches. Cut a felt strip for the belt measuring 4 inches wide by the desired waist measurement minus 8 inches. (If your waist is 26 inches, for example, cut felt rectangle to measure 4 by 16½ inches.) Cut a second felt strip 2 inches wide by the same length. Position the 2 felt strips with the 2-inch-wide strip exactly in the middle, as shown in *Diagram 5-C2.*

DIAGRAM 5-C2

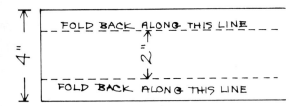

6. To give the belt some body, fold bottom and top of wider strip over, so that they meet in the center of the 2-inch strip, and glue in place to secure. Cover with waxed paper or aluminum foil and press with heavy books. Let dry completely.

7. Push the tab on the mouth of 1 of the fish through the curtain ring from front to back, and glue on back to secure it. Lay belt out with seam face down, and glue this fish to 1 end, allowing a 1-inch overlap. (See *Diagram 5-C3.*)

8. Cut nylon fastening tape in half. Glue 1 piece of nylon fastening tape to the back of the tab on the other fish's mouth. Slip tab through ring from front to back to find position on the back of this fish's body for the corresponding piece of fastening tape, and glue it in place. Glue this fish to the other end of the belt.

DIAGRAM 5-C3

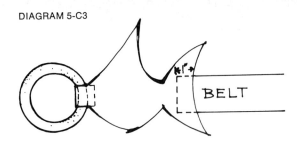

BACK VIEW

9. Glue 2 horizontal rows of rickrack about ½ inch apart down the length of the belt. Let all glue dry thoroughly.

10. To wear belt, attach the nylon fastening tape pieces.

Seashell Belt

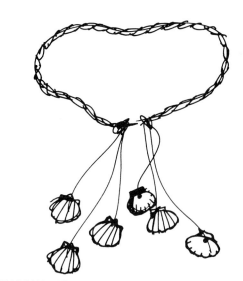

DIAGRAM 5-DD

The next time you are at the seashore, remember to collect some shells to use on this belt. Try to select ones that are fairly thin and uniform in size. Because you have to pierce a small hole in the top of each shell to fasten it to the leather ties of the belt, you may break a few shells, so be sure to collect several extras. This is an inexpensive, attractive project to make for a bazaar, and you should start collecting seashells early in the season in order to have lots of material on hand for future belts.

MATERIALS

6 or more thin, flat seashells (scallop, clam, etc.), 2½ inches wide or in diameter
shellac
1 paintbrush
3 leather thongs, approximately 50 inches long, ⅛ inch wide
1 old bath towel
1 brad (thin nail), 1 inch long
hammer

1. Brush shells on 1 side with shellac. Let dry. Turn over and shellac the other side. Let dry.

2. Knot the 3 leather strands together 9 inches in from 1 end. Braid strands together to within 10 inches of the other end.

3. Tie another knot to secure the braiding, and set aside.

4. Lay seashells on folded bath towel to help cushion them while you pierce the holes. The hole

in each shell should be large enough to permit the leather strip to pass through; make it about ¼ inch in from the center top of the shell. Position nail point where the hole is to go and strike nail firmly with hammer. It may be necessary to punch 2 or 3 small holes together to make 1 hole large enough for the thong to go through.

5. Tie seashells onto the 3 strands on 1 end of the belt. Tie 1 seashell to 1 strand 6 inches from the braiding, 1 to the second strand at 4 inches, and 1 to the third at 2 inches. Cut away excess thong. Repeat for the other end of the belt. (See *Diagram 5-D1.*)

6. To wear, tie belt around waist or hip.

Bangle Belt

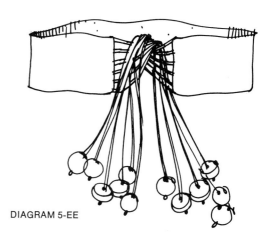

DIAGRAM 5-EE

Wooden curtain rings, wooden rings from a child's broken toy, large wooden beads, or large, painted wooden thread spools can be used to make this jangly belt. Glue, scissors, and possibly some paint are the only tools you'll need.

MATERIALS

½ yard fabric-backed vinyl, in any desired color
white resin glue
12 wooden rings, large beads, or large spools
1 small jar acrylic paint, to match or contrast with vinyl

DIAGRAM 5-D1

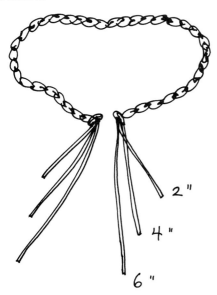

2 "

4 "

6 "

DIAGRAM 5-E1

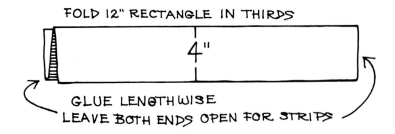

FOLD 12" RECTANGLE IN THIRDS

4"

GLUE LENGTHWISE
LEAVE BOTH ENDS OPEN FOR STRIPS

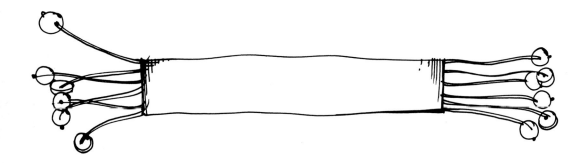

1. Cut vinyl into a rectangle 12 inches wide and as long as your waist measurement minus 4 inches. Since the belt is cut shorter than waist measurement, the ties will cross in front when you wear it.

2. Fold rectangle in thirds lengthwise, with vinyl facing out, and glue lengthwise to secure. Do not glue shut the short ends of the folded belt. (See *Diagram 5-E1.*)

3. From remaining vinyl cut 12 strips each measuring 11 inches by ¾ inch.

4. Fold each 11-inch strip in half lengthwise, with vinyl facing out, to form a narrow doubled strip. Glue to secure and let dry completely.

5. Dot 1 end of each of the 6 strips with glue. Insert them evenly in opening at 1 end of the belt, pushing the glued ends 1 inch in to secure. Repeat with other 6 strips at other end of the belt. Let dry completely.

6. If you are using unpainted rings or spools, you may want to paint them first, in a color to match or contrast with the belt. Let dry.

7. Knot 1 ring or spool onto each of the 12 belt ties.

8. To wear, knot ties together in center.

Chain-Latch Belt

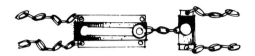

DIAGRAM 5-FF

I got the idea for this project one day when I was painting the kitchen. All the hardware had been removed to keep it from being splattered with paint. As I looked at a chain latch lying on the kitchen counter, I thought, "That would make a nifty belt!" So I tried it.

MATERIALS

1 brass chain door lock, 7 to 9 inches when chain is pulled taut
2 lengths lightweight gold metal chain (length of each determined by hip measurement minus 7- to 9-inch allowance for door lock)
pliers

1. Attach 1 end of each lightweight chain to 1 side of the door lock, using pliers to open chain links and close them after inserting through 1 of the 2 screw holes of the lock.
2. Repeat on the other end of the lock with the other ends of the 2 chains.
3. To wear, slide 1 part of lock into other as you would to lock a door. Wear around hips.

Cupboard-Hinge Belt

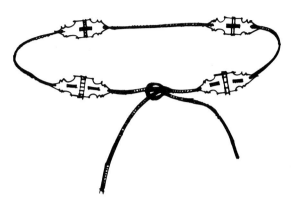

DIAGRAM 5-GG

Here's an instant belt that has all the impact of a designer belt for a fraction of the price. If your club or bazaar is looking for an easy item to make for its annual sale, this is it.

MATERIALS

4 brass cupboard hinges, approximately ½ by 2½ inches
1 leather thong (if the hinges have a double row of screw holes, use 2 thongs), approximately 50 inches long

1. Thread the leather thong through the screw holes of all 4 cupboard hinges.
2. Position the 4 hinges evenly around the belt about 8 inches apart.
3. Tie ends of leather thong to wear.

Suede-Cloth Belt

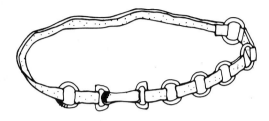

DIAGRAM 5-HH

Cotton suede cloth, which is easier to work with than real suede and a lot less expensive, too, makes this smartly tailored belt in double-quick time.

MATERIALS

⅛ yard suede cloth

white resin glue

1 brass belt buckle, 2-piece link style, with 1-inch metal rod

5 to 7 brass cafe curtain rings (without hooks), 1½-inch diameter

several spring-type clothespins or 1-inch metal hairclips

1. Cut suede cloth into 5 rectangles, each 3 by 3½ inches. For a waist measurement of 30 inches or more, cut 1 or more additional rectangles as needed.

2. Fold each rectangle in thirds lengthwise to form a 3-layered rectangle 1 by 3½ inches, and glue along outer side to secure. Let dry completely. (See *Diagram 5-H1.*)

DIAGRAM 5-H1

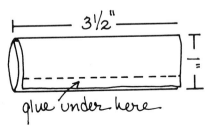

3. Loop 1 suede-cloth strip through half of the buckle and 1 brass curtain ring. Bring the 2 ends of the suede cloth together on the wrong side, overlap them ¼ inch, and glue in place. (See *Diagram 5-H2.*) Use a clothespin or hairclip to hold

DIAGRAM 5-H2

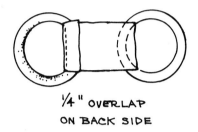

¼" OVERLAP ON BACK SIDE

the overlap while the glue is drying. Loop the second suede-cloth strip through the opposite side of the same curtain ring and another curtain ring, overlap ¼ inch on the wrong side, and glue as before. Continue in the same manner until at least 5 rings are in place.

4. The amount of suede cloth necessary for the remainder of the belt will depend on the size of either your hips or waist. Try on as much of the belt as you have completed, and measure yourself to determine the remaining number of inches required to make the buckle ends meet. Where you want the belt to fall is up to you.

5. Cut a piece of suede cloth 3 inches wide and the length needed to complete belt. Fold this piece into thirds lengthwise as you did with the shorter pieces in step 2, and glue to secure. A few heavy books protected by waxed paper or aluminum foil can be used to hold in place until glue sets. Let dry completely. Then loop this long strip through the last curtain ring and the other part of the belt buckle, overlapping ¼ inch on wrong side, and glue to secure.

Scalloped Evening Belt

DIAGRAM 5-II

By using an elaborate gold and rhinestone button for the buckle of this belt, you will have the effect of a fancy buckle that costs upward of $3 for a third of the cost.

MATERIALS

1 package wide rickrack, in gold
1 felt strip (length determined by waist measurement
plus 2 inches) 1½ inches wide, in white
white resin glue
thread in white
1 fancy gold and rhinestone button, 1- to 1½-inch
diameter
2 inches nylon fastening tape

1. Remove rickrack from package and press to remove creases. Set iron on low, for synthetics and rayon.

2. Fold felt strip in half lengthwise so that it measures ¾ inch wide. Press on fold and glue to secure.

3. Cut 2 strips of rickrack the length of the felt plus an additional 2 or 3 inches.

4. Pin the 2 strips of rickrack together at end. Intertwine the strips by placing 1 piece over and then under the other. Work on an ironing board, pinning rickrack down as you work. It will pucker slightly; press it flat with iron at low setting.

5. Glue rickrack to center of the felt strip. Let dry completely.

6. Fold 1 end of the belt under ½ inch, and sew the button to the outside of the belt right over

this folded ½ inch, taking stitches through all layers. Fold the other end of the belt under ½ inch and stitch or glue in place.

7. Sew a piece of nylon fastening tape directly under the button on the wrong side and to the outside face of the other end of the belt.

Cleopatra Collar

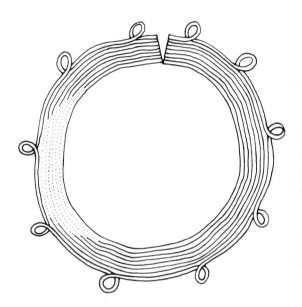

DIAGRAM 5-JJ

I made this dramatic gold collar one morning in 25 minutes while I was having my coffee! Cost to make? Less than 50 cents!

MATERIALS

compass
felt rectangles, 9 by 12 inches, in any desired color
1 spool gift-tie cord, 20 feet, in gold
white resin glue
1 inch nylon fastening tape, ½ inch wide

1. Using a compass, draw an 8-inch-diameter circle on the felt, and cut out.

98

2. Place the compass point in the exact center and draw a 7-inch-diameter circle for the base of the collar.

3. Begin to glue cord on the inner edge of the circle. First apply enough glue for 2 rows of cord.

4. Glue the first and second rows of cord flush against each other all the way around the felt. Work in a continuous spiral. Apply more glue and continue spiraling cord in the same manner until 7 rows are completed. Press down gently to get the cord to lie flat.

5. On the eighth row make a small loop of about 1 inch of cord every 2½ inches around the edge of the collar, adding a tiny extra spot of glue at the point where the loop intersects. This creates a lacy edge. (See *Diagram 5-J1*.) Let dry.

DIAGRAM 5-J1

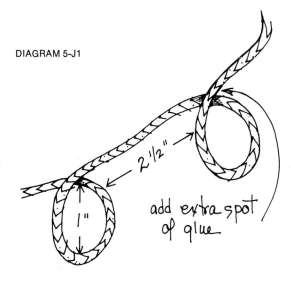

6. Slash the collar at any point by cutting through the rows of cord from the outside to the inside of the circle.

7. Glue nylon fastening tape closure to the bottom of 1 end of the collar and to the top of the other end to form a closure at the back of the neck.

Instant Beaded Choker

DIAGRAM 5-KK

This instant party accessory has real dash for about a third of the cash you'd have to pay for a similar ready-made choker. Splurge on the most luxurious trim you can find, because even though beaded trim is expensive, you'll need only an amount equal to your neck measurement plus ½ inch. Don't overlook the possibility of making a matching bracelet while you're at it.

MATERIALS

elaborate beaded trim (length determined by neck measurement plus ½ inch), ½ inch wide
thread to match trim
2 hooks and eyes

Turn raw ends of trim under ¼ inch, and secure with a few tiny stitches so that the beads will not unravel. Since most beaded trims have a very soft, thin, cotton base, you need do nothing more than sew on 2 hooks and eyes at each end of the choker.

Sparkle Chain

DIAGRAM 5-LL

Here's a dangly necklace to make for holiday events or other special occasions. You'll be surprised at being able to achieve such elegance in less than an hour and at a cost of less than a dollar!

MATERIALS

1 crochet hook, size #9

1 spool nonelastic metallic thread (there'll be lots left over for other projects), in gold

1 bag paillettes, approximately 100 pieces, in assorted colors

1. With #9 crochet hook and gold metallic thread, chain 12. For the next chain, slip a paillette onto the hook, and crochet through it just as though you were chaining without a paillette on the hook. Continue to add a paillette on every thirteenth chain or every inch.

2. Repeat until all paillettes are used, or until desired length is reached. Join the first chain stitch to the last stitch of chain by knotting securely. Weave ends through a few stitches and cut off excess.

3. To wear, wind around neck 3 or 4 times.

Variation: All by itself without paillettes, this simple chain is one of the most versatile pieces of jewelry you can own. With any charm, bauble, or watch hung from it, it looks almost like a gold metal chain. To wear as the foundation for a pendant, crochet a 22- or 24-inch length of chain and join as described in step 2 above.

Photograph Pendant

DIAGRAM 5-MM

1. Place curtain ring on photograph so that subject's head is centered, and trace around inside of curtain ring. Cut out photograph on traced line.

2. Cut felt circle ⅛ inch larger in diameter than the photograph.

3. Glue back of photograph to felt circle, leaving ⅛-inch felt border all around.

4. Apply glue to this ⅛-inch border and press curtain ring over it, making sure that the loop on the curtain ring is at the center top of the photograph. Let dry completely.

5. Use pliers to open the loop in order to attach pendant to metal or gold crocheted neck chain.

Romantic Pleated Collar

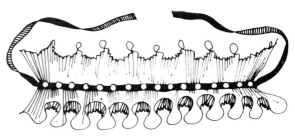

DIAGRAM 5-NN

This collar takes only ten minutes to construct. A ruffled collar is perfect for the times when you yearn to be just a little romantic. I wear it over a long-sleeved black sweater, but if you prefer pastels, choose velvet ribbon in a color to match whatever you plan to wear it with.

For a cost of practically pennies, you can create this photograph pendant to wear on any metal chain—or the gold crocheted chain described in the preceding project. Several of these pendants could be hung on a link bracelet to make a charm bracelet; for this variation use smaller curtain rings and photographs than called for in the instructions below.

MATERIALS

1 brass curtain ring with extra loop, 2-inch diameter
1 color photograph (subject's head should be 1 to 1½ inches in size)
felt, 3 by 3 inches, in any desired color
white resin glue
pliers

MATERIALS

1 yard pleated nylon trim (finished on 1 edge only), 2 inches wide, or ½ yard pleated nylon trim (finished on both edges), 4 inches wide
white resin glue
2 yards velvet ribbon, ¼ inch wide, in black
30 to 35 rhinestones or pearls, ¼-inch diameter (optional)
1 beading needle (optional)
thread in black (optional)

1. (If you are working with the 4-inch trim, omit this step and proceed to step 2.) Cut trim into pieces, each ½ yard long, and glue them together along their length, making sure to overlap the edges ¼ inch. Let dry.

2. Center velvet ribbon on pleated trim so that equal lengths of ribbon extend at each end for neck ties. Glue ribbon down the exact center of trim.

3. If desired, tack a pearl or rhinestone every ½ inch across the ribbon, using beading needle and black thread. Do not put beads on neck ties.

4. To wear, tie ribbon in a bow at the back of the neck.

Beaded "Leather" Choker

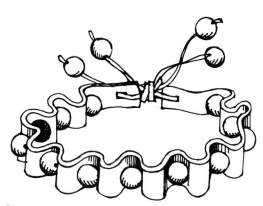

DIAGRAM 5-OO

This choker was designed as a project for teenagers to make. It can also be made with felt or vinyl, instead of leather. Extended to waist length, this design would make an attractive belt.

MATERIALS

18 inches imitation leather or felt, ½ inch wide, in any desired color
1 large darning needle
heavy-duty thread to match imitation leather or felt
28 wooden beads, ½-inch diameter
1 leather thong, cut to two 12-inch lengths, or two 12-inch felt strips, ¼ inch wide

1. Cut a length of thread 40 inches long. Thread needle, double thread, and knot ends together.

2. Insert needle up into the large "leather" or felt piece about 1½ inches in from 1 end, leaving knot on the bottom of the fabric.

3. String a bead onto the thread, and then go down through the fabric with your needle, allowing just enough space for the bead. With needle on bottom, string another bead, and come up through the fabric to top side. Continue in this manner, having succeeding beads on alternate sides of fabric, until 4 beads are left and you are 1½ inches from the end of the fabric. Set remaining beads aside. (See *Diagram 5-O1.*)

DIAGRAM 5-O1

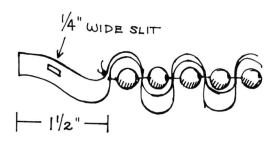

4. Secure thread on the wrong side of the fabric with a knot. Cut excess thread off very close to knot.

5. With scissors, cut a tiny horizontal slit (about ¼ inch) in the middle of both ends of the strip ½ inch in from each end. (See *Diagram 5-O1.*)

6. Fold 1 piece of leather thong or strip of felt in half. Slip folded end through one ¼-inch slit on the choker, and pass the cut ends through the folded end to form neck ties. Repeat with other strip at other end of choker.

7. Knot a bead onto each of the 4 ends of the 2 neck ties, and tie around neck to wear.

Traveling Jewelry Case

5-P1. Fold edge A-A' up to meet B-B'. Glue ½ inch along edges. Let dry.

DIAGRAM 5-P1

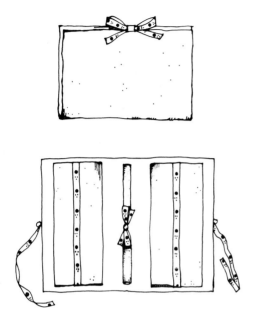

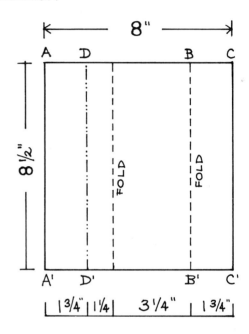

DIAGRAM 5-PP

This crushable, easy-to-pack jewelry case makes a lovely gift. It has lots of room in which to store all shapes and sizes of baubles.

MATERIALS

¼ yard felt, in any desired color, or 7 felt rectangles, 9 by 12 inches, all 1 color

white resin glue

2 yards embroidered trim, ½ inch wide

5 pieces nylon fastening tape, 1 inch long

thread to match felt

1. Cut felt pieces in the following sizes: 1 rectangle 9 by 12 inches, 2 rectangles 8 by 8½ inches, 2 squares 3 by 3 inches.

2. Cut trim in the following lengths: 2 strips 8½ inches long, 2 strips 5 inches long, 2 strips 8 inches long.

3. Fold one 8- by 8½-inch piece of felt, envelope style, in unequal thirds, as shown in *Diagram*

4. Fold edge C-C' over doubled thickness of fabric to D-D' to create envelope flap. Glue 1 piece of nylon fastening tape on inside center of flap and another piece of tape to corresponding part of felt envelope.

5. Repeat steps 3 and 4 with second 8- by 8½-inch felt rectangle to make a second envelope.

6. Glue back of 1 envelope at each end of 9- by 12-inch felt rectangle, as shown in *Diagram 5-P2.*

7. Glue one 8½-inch strip of trim over 1 envelope flap edge, as shown in *Diagram 5-P2.* Repeat for other envelope.

8. Spread glue lightly over 1 side of each 3- by 3-inch square and roll to form a cylinder ½ inch in diameter; these will become rods for rings.

9. Sew a 5-inch strip of trim to 1 end of 1 ring rod; repeat with other 5-inch strip of trim and other rod.

DIAGRAM 5-P2

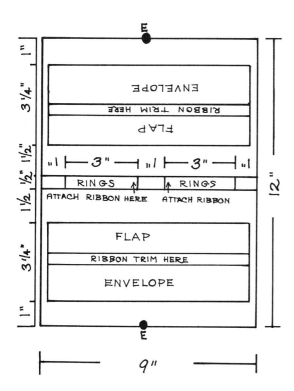

Butterfly Hair Ornament

DIAGRAM 5-QQ

This glittery, shimmery butterfly is especially pretty when worn with long hair or a French twist.

MATERIALS

1 sheet tracing paper
1 felt rectangle, 9 by 12 inches, in any desired color
thread to match felt
25 pearls, ¼-inch diameter
25 pearls, ⅛-inch diameter
10 (approximately) paillettes, in gold
1 package small oval beads, gold-plated (available at a fabric or trimming store)
10 to 12 small cosmetic cotton balls
¾ yard metallic trim, ¼ inch wide, in gold
1 small plastic comb, approximately 2 by 2 inches

1. Trace butterfly shape from *Diagram 5-Q1;* cut out and pin on felt.

2. Cut out 2 butterfly shapes from felt.

3. Sew pearls, paillettes, and gold beads at random over the top of the butterfly only. Do not sew anything on the outer ¼ inch, where gold trim will be applied later.

4. Place the 2 butterflies together, and over-cast them along the edges by hand, leaving 2

10. Use needle and thread to tack the end of each rod that does not have trim attached to 1 outer edge of the 9- by 12-inch felt rectangle, as shown in *Diagram 5-P2.* Ring rods go in the exact center of piece as folded crosswise. Tie trim in a bow between ring rods.

11. Sew an 8-inch strip of trim to each side of jewelry case at E. Tie in a bow to close case.

inches open at the top center, as shown in *Diagram 5-Q1.*

5. Push cotton balls through the top opening and into the wings and body of the butterfly. Sew up the top opening by hand.

6. Glue metallic trim all around the edge of the butterfly.

7. Sew haircomb to the wrong side of the hair ornament. Insert comb in hair to wear.

DIAGRAM 5-Q1

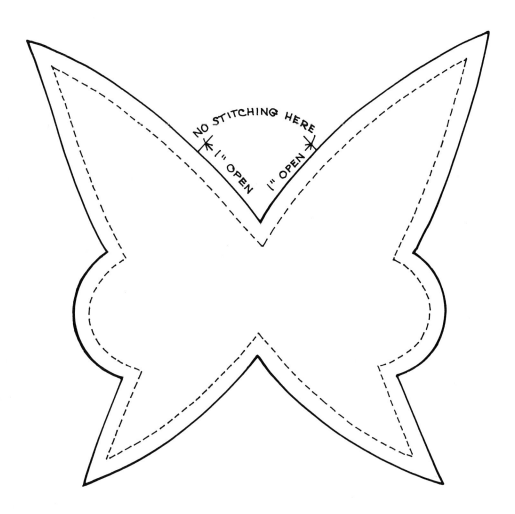

Fabric-covered Barrettes

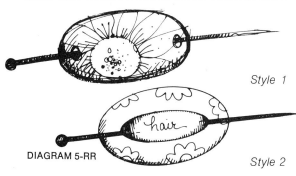

Style 1

Style 2

DIAGRAM 5-RR

Cut from an empty plastic bottle such as bleach comes in, these barrettes can be made for pennies. They are a good project for Brownie or Girl Scout troops, since they are not hard to make and—best of all—girls will adore wearing them. Diagrams illustrate two different styles.

MATERIALS

1 empty plastic bleach bottle
tracing paper
felt-tipped marker
fabric scraps (felt, cotton, vinyl)
white resin glue
orangewood stick (used for manicures) or swizzle stick (with rounded end)

1. *Style 1:* With scissors, cut away the top and the bottom of the bottle to leave a cylinder. Cut down side seam to make a flat piece of plastic.

2. Flatten the piece of plastic. Don't worry if it doesn't lie completely flat, since it must be slightly curved for these barrettes.

3. Trace designs from *Diagram 5-R1*, or create your own. Cut out. Place paper pattern on plastic and draw around it with felt-tipped marker. Cut out plastic barrette shape.

4. Cut 2 pieces of fabric to correspond to the plastic form, making 1 for the barrette top, ¼ inch *larger* all around, and the other, for the barrette bottom, ⅛ inch *smaller* all around.

5. Glue the larger fabric piece to the top (outward curving side) of the plastic. Pull the ¼-inch border of fabric over the edges and onto the back of the barrette and glue. Cover the raw edges by gluing the smaller fabric piece to the back. Let dry completely.

6. With scissors or an ice pick, carefully make a small hole (about ¼-inch diameter) ¼ inch in from each side of the barrette. (See *Diagram 5-RR,* style 1.)

7. To wear, insert orangewood stick or swizzle stick through hole in the barrette, under the hair, and out through the hole on the other side.

8. *Style 2:* Repeat steps 1 through 5, following *Diagram 5-R1* for style 2.

9. Insert orangewood or swizzle stick through the barrette and pull hair through barrette, as shown in sketch.

DIAGRAM 5-R1

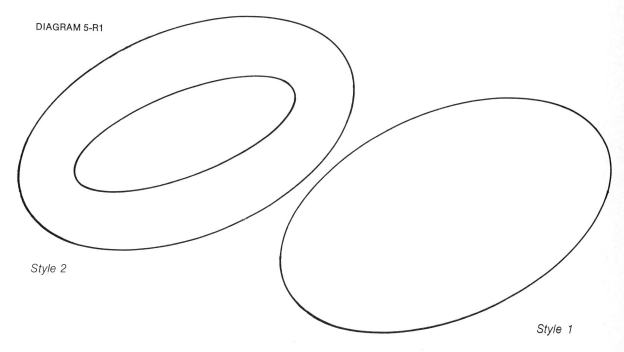

Style 2

Style 1

Belt Headband

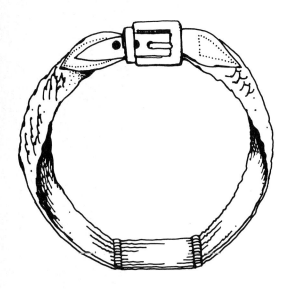

DIAGRAM 5-SS

A narrow belt that no longer fits, or one that you're tired of, may easily be converted into an attractive headband in just a few minutes.

MATERIALS

1 narrow belt
4 inches elastic, ¼ inch wide
heavy-duty thread

1. Close belt buckle. Cut belt off 6 inches from the center of the buckle on each side.
2. Sew 1 end of the elastic to each cut end of belt, taking a few stitches in place to secure.

Felt Buttons and Flowers

DIAGRAM 5-TT

These buttons and flowers are versatile decorative additions to everything from hair-dos to shoes!

Toggle Buttons

The technique for making these buttons is the same as for making crescent rolls! I first made them to perk up a plain felt tunic made from a commercial pattern. Enlarge the button pattern slightly, make two of them in leather, and, voila— shoe buckles! I use the metal clips that fasten clothes returned to me by the dry cleaner to fasten them to my shoes.

MATERIALS

1 sheet tracing paper
⅛ yard felt or 1 felt rectangle, 9 by 12 inches, or felt scraps
white resin glue
1 set snaps for each button
thread to match felt

1. Trace triangle from *Diagram 5-T1;* cut out. Pin to felt and cut 1 pattern piece for each button desired.
2. Starting at the wide end, roll triangle, adding a few drops of glue as you roll. Press with fingers to secure and let dry completely.
3. Sew buttons to garments as desired.
4. To close garment, sew a snap directly under each button and to the corresponding point on the other side of garment.

DIAGRAM 5-T1

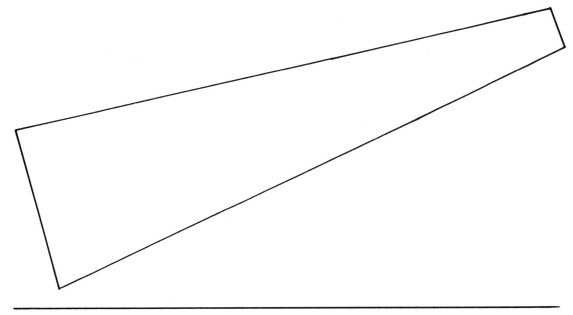

Roses

DIAGRAM 5-UU

These felt roses are a cinch to make and provide an unusual trim for any hat, purse, or skirt. They also can be glued or clipped to a pair of plain pumps (use metal clips from the dry cleaner). One felt rose glued to a metal hairclip makes a lovely barrette or hair ornament.

MATERIALS

felt, 1¼ by 11 inches (a 9- by 12-inch felt rectangle
will make 7 roses), in any desired color
11 inches grosgrain ribbon, 1 inch wide, to match felt
for each rose
heavy-duty thread to match felt

1. With scissors, round the bottom ends of felt strip, as shown in *Diagram 5-U1*.

2. Place grosgrain ribbon on top of felt strip. Fold and pin the ends of the ribbon under slightly to form a curve. Do not round the ribbon corners, as they may fray. Using a needle and double thread, gather both pieces together ¼ inch in from the edge along the long, straight (uncurved) side.

3. Pull thread as tightly as possible; knot to secure. Do not cut off thread.

4. Roll the flower from 1 end to the other, and tack with 2 or 3 stitches to secure.

5. Sew or glue completed flower to hat, skirt, or purse.

DIAGRAM 5-U1

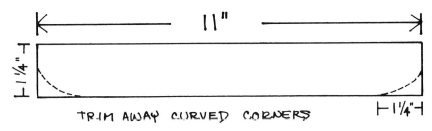

TRIM AWAY CURVED CORNERS

Daisies

DIAGRAM 5-VV

Felt daisies add a perky touch to any hat, which is the way I've shown them here. They are also effective for any of the uses suggested above. In addition, you can try them on a pocketbook, a child's jumper, or a hostess skirt.

MATERIALS

1 sheet tracing paper
1 felt rectangle, 9 by 12 inches (will make 5 flowers), in any desired color
1 spool wire, size #28
white resin glue
5 balls from ½-inch ball fringe (for flower centers) in contrasting color

1. Trace petal shape from *Diagram 5-V1;* cut out. Pin to felt and cut out as many as desired. Note that 5 petals are required for 1 flower.

DIAGRAM 5-V1

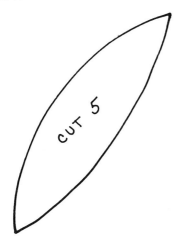

2. Fold each petal in half lengthwise. Stack 5 folded petals together, 1 on top of another, with all folds facing the same way. Tie together tightly across the exact center with a 3-inch piece of wire. (See *Diagram 5-V2.*) Twist to secure, but do

DIAGRAM 5-V2

not cut the wire. Fan the petals out into a circle resembling a daisy.

3. Glue 1 ball from ball fringe to the center of each flower.

4. To trim hat as shown: Glue ball fringe to match flower centers around brim. Use 3 felt rectangles and about ¾ yard ball fringe to make about 15 flowers to scatter at random over hat. Push wire on the flowers through the body of the hat and attach to the underside of the crown or brim. Twist ends of wire to secure flower to hat; cut off any excess wire close to hat. Push tiny ends of wire to inside of hat.

6
Handbags
and Hats

Velvet Evening Bag

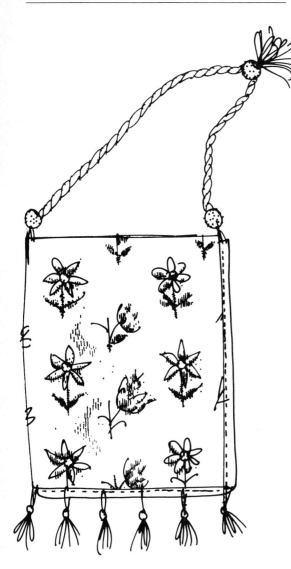

2 pieces cut velvet upholstery fabric, each 12 by 15 inches
thread to match fabric
white resin glue
6 small drapery tassels, 5 inches long, to match fabric
1 drapery tieback, to match tassels

1. Place both fabric pieces together with right sides facing, and stitch or glue on 1 short end and both long ends. Let dry completely.

2. Turn right side out. Fold top (unglued or unstitched) edges of the purse to inside for 1 inch, and glue or stitch.

3. Tack drapery tassels, evenly spaced, across the bottom edge of the purse.

4. Sew drapery tieback ends to opposite sides on the outside of the top of the purse to form a handle, as shown in *Diagram 6-AA*.

DIAGRAM 6-AA

Cut or antique velvet upholstery fabric always looks elegant, and remnants are often available for a dollar or two. The silk drapery tassels that trim this purse look expensive too, but they'll probably cost less than $2—you'll have a luxurious purse at a bargain price.

Woven Purse

DIAGRAM 6-BB

This smartly tailored design, which can easily be completed in about an hour, is an ideal traveler. It takes up very little room in a suitcase but expands to hold quite a lot of gear.

MATERIALS

¼ yard felt, in each of 2 contrasting colors
1 bath towel (optional)
white resin glue
thread to match 1 of the felt pieces

1. Cut a 12- by 24-inch rectangle from the color of felt you wish to be dominant. Pin it to a flat surface, such as an ironing board or a bath towel placed on a table.

2. From the same color felt, cut 8 strips 24 inches long by 1½ inches wide.

3. From the contrasting color felt, cut 13 strips 12 inches long by 1½ inches wide.

4. Cut 2 felt strips (1 of each color) 24 inches long by 2 inches wide for the purse handle.

5. Cut a felt band 2 inches wide by 22 inches long from either color to bind the inside of the purse.

6. Pin the 8 strips from step 2 to the large felt piece at 1 narrow end (top) only. (See *Diagram 6-B1.*)

DIAGRAM 6-B1

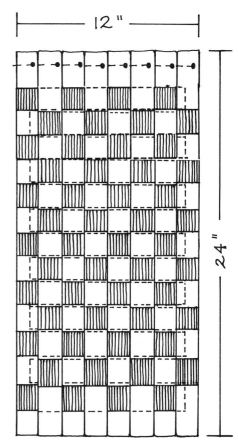

7. Pin the 13 strips from step 3 to the large felt piece at 1 long end (side). Starting with the top strip of this group, weave it across, over and under the longer strips, pinning it when you get to the end of the row.

8. Continue weaving the 11-inch strips, in alternating over-and-under pattern, until all strips are woven and pinned at both sides. Pin bottoms of long strips in place to hold.

9. Glue or topstitch ¼ inch from edge to hold all weaving strip ends to large felt piece, removing pins as you go. If glued, let dry before going on to next step.

10. Fold large felt piece in half crosswise with woven sides together. Pin along sides to hold. Seam sides together by hand or machine, ½ inch in from each edge, removing pins as you sew.

11. Stitch diagonally across each bottom corner, as shown in *Diagram 6-B2.*

DIAGRAM 6-B2

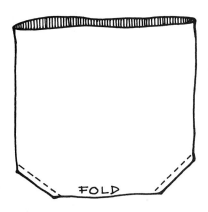

12. Turn purse right side out.

13. Place handle strips from step 4 together, 1 on top of the other, and glue or topstitch. If glued, let dry.

14. Glue or stitch 1 end of the handle to each side of the purse at the top.

15. Turn top edges in for 1½ inches and glue to secure. Glue the felt band from step 5 on the inside top to cover this edge.

Oriental Carpetbag

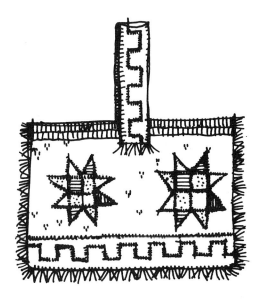

DIAGRAM 6-CC

Ready-made carpetbags are quite expensive; most do-it-yourself versions are complicated and all are bulky and clunky to carry. This version is as flat as a pancake, is simple to make, and holds a lot. Try making it from an old, worn-out Oriental rug. You can cut around the torn spots and color in any bare spots with waterproof felt-tipped markers. Your rug need not be an Oriental; any nubby or flat, plain or patterned, rug will do.

MATERIALS

3 pieces of carpet: 2 pieces 12 by 14 inches and 1 piece 3½ by 18 inches
several thin nails or heavy straight pins
heavy-duty polyester thread to match carpet
1 heavy carpet needle
felt-tipped markers (optional)

1. If there is a design on your carpet, try to center it before cutting the 12- by 14-inch rectangles. Use a nail or straight pin to fringe ½ inch of the sides and bottoms of both pieces. Place both pieces with wrong sides together, and overcast by hand between fringe on sides and bottom.

2. Fringe narrow strip of carpet (bag handle) on the short ends only. Finish long raw edges of the handle by overcasting.

3. Sew 1 end of handle to center of front of bag; sew other end to center of back of bag, as shown in sketch.

Picture Purse

DIAGRAM 6-DD

After my first child was born, I was never without a photograph of her. But as two more children came along, I grew lax about carrying their pic-

tures with me, even though there were times when I wanted to show them off. This purse guarantees that photographs of the children will always be on hand. It's a good way to rejuvenate an old purse, too!

MATERIALS

1 wicker purse with flat top or flat side
1 small can acrylic paint, in any desired color
1 paintbrush
1 wood picture frame, 3 by 4 inches
1 photograph to fit frame
white resin glue

1. Remove any existing trim on the purse. Brush with acrylic paint and let dry completely. Apply a second coat of paint if necessary and let dry.

2. Paint wood picture frame in the same color and let dry.

3. Cut photograph to fit and insert in frame.

4. Glue the back of the frame to the top or side of the purse, whichever is most suitable. Let dry.

Grandmother's Purse

DIAGRAM 6-EE

Although my children's grandmother has many purses and tote bags, none is more special to her than this one, which shows all sixteen members of the family on it. Perhaps she treasures it so highly because it allows her to brag about her family without having to be so obvious as to pull out a raft of photographs.

MATERIALS

tracing paper

1 felt rectangle, 9 by 12 inches, in green

1 flat-sided straw, wicker, or canvas bag, about 12 by 12 inches

white resin glue

color snapshots of individual members of the family (heads should all be about the same size, roughly the size of a quarter)

1 package gift-wrap cord, 25 feet, in gold

1 small spool wire, size #28

1. Trace family tree as shown in *Diagram 6-E1* (or draw your own) and cut out. Pin to the green felt rectangle; draw outline and cut out.

2. Glue family tree in the center of 1 side of the purse.

3. Cut out heads of family members from photographs, tracing around a quarter to get a perfect circle. Glue photo circles directly onto leaves and trunk of the tree.

4. Make picture frames for each photo: Cut gold cord into as many 4-inch pieces as there are photos. Cut wire into an equal number of 3½-inch pieces. Push a piece of wire into center of each piece of cord.

5. Bend each piece of wire-reinforced cord into a circle so that it just fits around the outside edge of each photo. Twist cord ends together once or twice where they join. Fray the ends of the cord above the twisted part for a tasseled ef-

fect and cut away any excess, leaving a frayed part of about ¼ inch. (See *Diagram 6-E2.*)

6. Carefully glue frame to outside edge of photograph. Be careful not to get glue on photographs. Tasseled part of frame should be at the center top of each photograph.

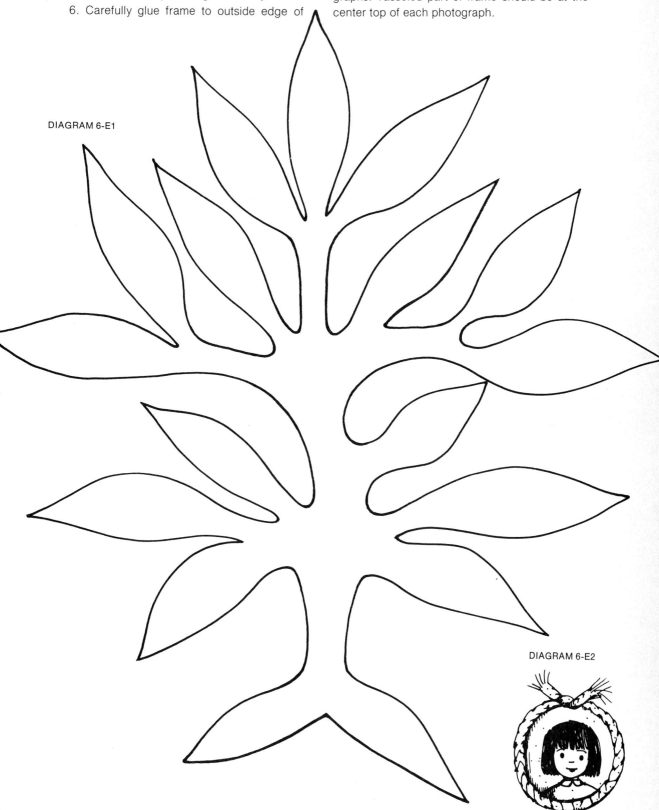

DIAGRAM 6-E1

DIAGRAM 6-E2

Pillow Tote

DIAGRAM 6-FF

MATERIALS

2 thin matching pillows, approximately 12 by 12 inches, in any desired color or pattern
heavy-duty polyester thread in white
1 set large snaps
24 inches upholstery cording, ¼-inch diameter
60 inches upholstery cording, ½-inch diameter

1. Place pillows together and overcast around 3 sides. The stitches will show but will be concealed later by upholstery cording.

2. Sew 1 snap half to the inside center of the open side of each pillow.

3. Sew the ¼-inch cording around both top sides of purse by hand.

4. Sew the ½-inch cording around the other 3 sides of the purse to conceal overcast stitches. Allow 1 yard of this cording to extend at the top of 1 side. Form shoulder strap by sewing the loose end of cording to the top of the opposite side.

5. If desired, finish off the tote handle by making 2 tassels from the ½-inch cording. Attach 1 tassel with a few stitches at each side of shoulder strap at the point where it joins the purse.

This decidedly different tote can easily be made in just over an hour if you begin with ready-made pillows. (It will take another hour or two if you make the pillows yourself.) To avoid a too-bulky look, do not use the fat, puffy kind but select knife-edge pillows that are not more than 2 inches thick. Patchwork pillows are especially pretty.

Super-strong Tote Bag

them ½ inch on the long edges, as shown in *Diagram 6-G1*. Let dry flat.

DIAGRAM 6-G1

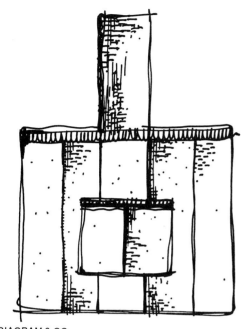

DIAGRAM 6-GG

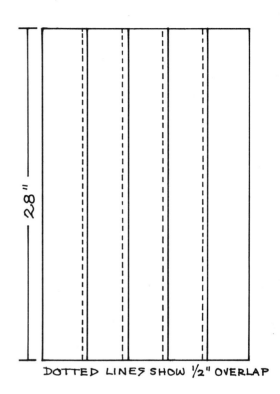

DOTTED LINES SHOW ½" OVERLAP

I discovered how strong this bag is while I was designing it. I glued together one version of the bag, but I wasn't satisfied with the result. When I tried to pull the glued pieces apart, it just couldn't be done. This super-strong tote would make a fine book bag for school-age youngsters. If you would like to add some decoration to the upholstery webbing, use waterproof felt-tipped markers or acrylic paints, and trace or stencil on it any design you like.

MATERIALS

3 yards upholstery webbing
white resin glue
1 yard fold-over cotton trim, ½-inch folded width

1. Cut upholstery webbing into 5 strips, 28 inches long, for the body of the tote. Cut 1 piece of webbing 20 inches long for the handle. Reserve remainder of the webbing.

2. Glue the 5 strips together, overlapping

3. Cut 2 strips of upholstery webbing, 8 inches long, for the pocket. Glue together, overlapping ½ inch on the long sides. Let dry flat.

4. Apply glue to both long sides of the body of tote bag, starting ½ inch down from the top and ending ½ inch up from the bottom. Fold in half crosswise to measure 14 inches deep with strips running vertically. Cover with waxed paper or aluminum foil and set heavy books over the folded piece. Let dry.

5. Cut 2 strips of fold-over trim to width of top of bag. Glue 1 over each top edge. Now, on both sides, glue together the ½ inch previously left

unglued, and again press with books or heavy weight until glue dries.

6. Glue 1 end of handle strip to the inside of the center strip on 1 side of the bag and the other handle end to the opposite center strip.

7. Cut fold-over trim to fit across the top of pocket plus 1 inch. Glue to pocket, turning ½ inch of trim under on each end.

8. Turn the untrimmed bottom edge of pocket under 1 inch. Glue sides and bottom edge of pocket to the front of the tote bag. Press bag under a layer of waxed paper and heavy books. Let glue dry thoroughly.

Strawberry Purse

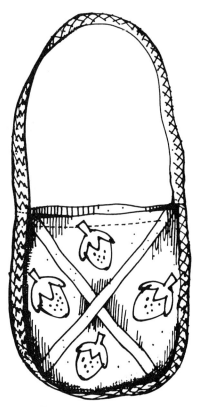

DIAGRAM 6-HH

Strawberry felt cutouts add a gay note to any garment or accessory. I'm partial to strawberries, and

here I've used them on one side of a purse that takes less than a half hour to complete. The red and green design is particularly pretty when placed on a background of navy, pink, or white.

MATERIALS

2 felt rectangles, 9 by 12 inches, or equivalent amount of any fabric with body, such as denim or vinyl, in any desired color
white resin glue
1½ yards woven hemp braid, 2 inches wide
thread to match purse fabric
1 sheet tracing paper
1 felt rectangle, 9 by 12 inches, in red
1 felt rectangle, 9 by 12 inches, in green
1 inch nylon fastening tape, 1 inch wide (optional)

1. Trim the two 9- by 12-inch felt rectangles for body of purse, as shown in *Diagram 6-H1*. Fold top edges under 1 inch and glue in place for hem.

DIAGRAM 6-H1

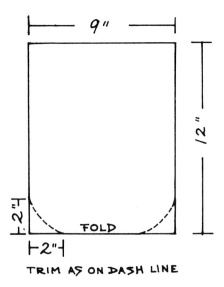

TRIM AS ON DASH LINE

2. To form the sides of the purse, pin the edge of the hemp braid to the edge of 1 side of the purse, starting from the center bottom. Right sides should be facing. Sew by hand or machine

¼ inch in from edge to the top of that side. Now join the other end of the hemp braid to the first end at the bottom center, overlapping ends by ½ inch, and sew it from bottom center up the other side to the top. (See *Diagram 6-H2.*)

DIAGRAM 6-H2

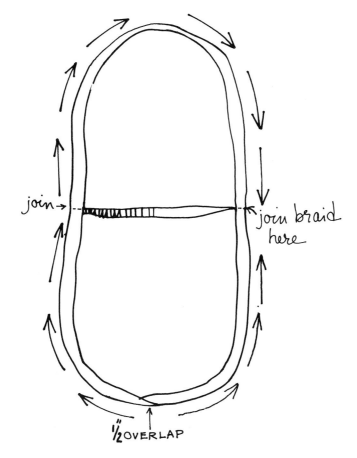

join → ← join braid here

½" OVERLAP

DIAGRAM 6-H3

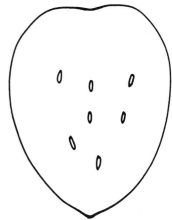

3. Join the other side of the purse to other side of hemp braid in the same manner, with right sides facing. Turn purse right side out. Use remaining braid for handle, joining ends where shown on *Diagram 6-H2.*

4. Trace strawberry design from *Diagram 6-H3;* cut out. Pin to red felt and cut out 4 times. Cut 2 red felt strips ½ by 12 inches to crisscross 1 side of the purse. Trim ends of strips diagonally. Glue in place and let dry.

5. Trace calyx (the green part atop each

berry) from *Diagram 6-H4;* cut out. Pin to green felt and cut out 4 times. Glue 1 calyx to the top of each strawberry. Glue completed berries on the bag, 1 in each of the 4 triangles formed by the intersecting red felt strips.

6. Glue nylon fastening tape to the top inside center of purse front and back to form a closure, if desired.

DIAGRAM 6-H4

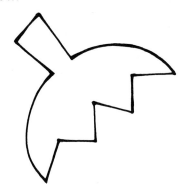

Calico Bandana Bag

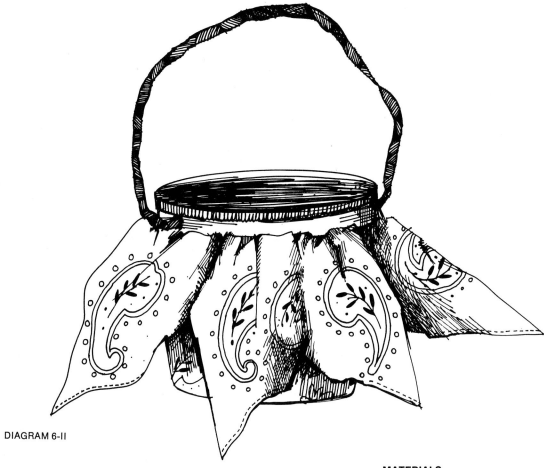

DIAGRAM 6-II

Because its base is a 2-quart round plastic container and it requires little more than one bandana-print kerchief, both from the dime store, this is a thrifty carryall for teen-age girls to make.

MATERIALS

1 cylindrical or bowl-shaped plastic container with round plastic top, 2-quart size
¼ yard felt, in black

white resin glue

¼ yard felt, in white

1 small jar or tube acrylic paint, in black

18 inches bulky acrylic gift-tie yarn, in black

1 cotton bandana-print scarf

6 inches (approximately) elastic, ¼ inch wide, or 1 large rubber band

1. Use tape measure to determine circumference of container. Measure depth of container. Cut a black felt rectangle to these measurements and glue in place to line the inside of the bag. Trace around base of container onto black felt and cut out; glue to inside to line bottom of container.

2. Cut the white felt in the same manner to fit the outside of the purse, adding 1 extra inch to the depth measurement to extend over the bottom edge, and glue all around the outside, and the edge of the purse's bottom. Trace, cut, and glue a circle of white felt to fit the bottom. Let dry completely.

3. Cut circles of black felt to fit the outside and the inside of the container lid, which will be the top of the bag. Glue felt circles to lid. Let dry. (See *Diagram 6-I1.*)

4. Paint the side edge of the lid with black acrylic paint. Let dry.

5. Use sharp scissors to punch small holes on opposite sides of the container ½ inch from the top. Push gift tie through holes for handle, knotting 1 end at the inside of each hole.

6. Place bandana flat on a table with right side facing you. Position container in the center of the bandana right side up. Pull all 4 corners of the bandana up, and secure with elastic around the container ½ inch below the top of the purse, taking a few stitches to hold the 2 ends of the elastic together (or use a rubber band). The right side of the bandana will flap over the elastic to show on the outside of the bag.

7. Snap on the lid and you're ready to go!

DIAGRAM 6-I1

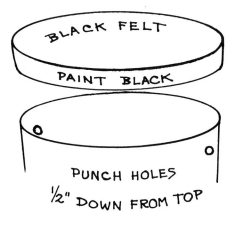

"Knit" Purse and Matching Beret

DIAGRAM 6-JJ

Do you have a tubular wool scarf you're tired of? Convert it to an unusual bag with matching beret. Actually, because most of these scarves are long enough to be wound several times round the neck, you might be able to make two bags and two berets from one. If so, give one set to your daughter to make a mother-daughter ensemble.

MATERIALS

1 tubular wool scarf, preferably with fringed ends
1 package rayon seam binding, to match scarf
thread to match scarf
**15 inches grosgrain ribbon, 1 inch wide, to match or
   contrast with scarf**

white resin glue
2 yards acrylic cording, ¼-inch diameter
compass
tailor's chalk pencil
**elastic (length determined by head measurement
   plus 1 inch), ¼ inch wide**

1. *Purse:* Cut 10 inches from 1 end of the scarf, as shown in *Diagram 6-J1.*

2. Separate the double-thickness of the scarf piece to make a pouch. Sew seam binding all around the new, single-thick raw edge. Turn under ½ inch at top of bag and sew in place all the way around.

3. Pin grosgrain ribbon on outside, 2½

DIAGRAM 6-J1

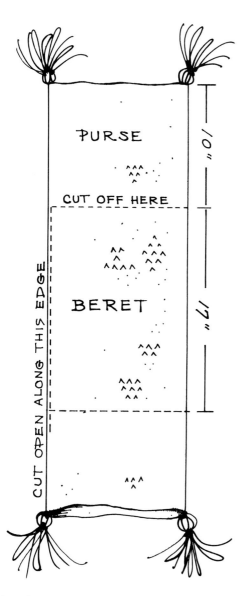

PURSE

10″

CUT OFF HERE

BERET

17″

CUT OPEN ALONG THIS EDGE

completely around, keeping it doubled, and out through first opening. Holding the loose ends, cut cording loop on fold. (See *Diagram 6-J2.*)

DIAGRAM 6-J2

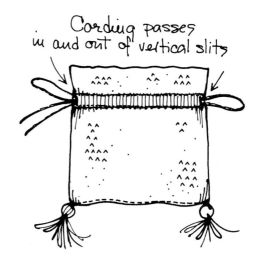

Cording passes in and out of vertical slits

5. There are now 2 cords in the casing. Knot opposite ends of each cord together, making 2 separate loops in casing. Pull 1 loop through opposite slit in casing.

6. Pull cording to close bag.

7. *Beret:* From raw edge on remaining piece of scarf, measure 17 inches and cut off. Cut open 1 side of this tubular section (See *Diagram 6-J1.*)

8. Use a compass with tailor's chalk pencil to draw a circle 16 inches in diameter on fabric; cut out.

9. Pin seam binding around edge of circle. Do not overlap ends; leave open. Stitch close to both edges of seam binding to form a casing.

10. Insert elastic through opening in casing. Pull through and overlap each end ½ inch; sew ends of the elastic together.

11. Press the beret lightly with a steam iron, using a pressing cloth.

inches down from the top all the way around. Sew close to top and bottom edges of ribbon to form a casing. Do not overlap or sew ends of ribbon; they should just meet and remain open for drawstring. Rub raw edges of ribbon ends lightly with glue to prevent fraying; let dry.

4. Fold cording in half and insert through casing. Cut a vertical slit in ribbon at the exact opposite side of bag from first ribbon opening (2 openings are needed for drawstring). Pull cording

Poncho Purse

DIAGRAM 6-KK

This thrifty idea converts a scuffed or soiled purse, or even an inexpensive plastic purse, to a unique poncho purse. The design looks best when made from a bag with a top zipper opening and a shoulder strap; a fabric with a plaid pattern is especially effective. Because purse sizes vary, you may have to adjust the measurements slightly.

MATERIALS

1 inexpensive or soiled purse

⅓ yard bonded wool or acrylic fabric or felt, at least 60 inches wide, in a pattern or solid color

2 yards ball fringe, in contrasting color

white resin glue

thread to match ball fringe (optional)

DIAGRAM 6-K1

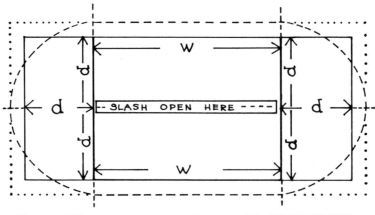

YOU NEED TWICE THE DEPTH IN <u>ALL</u> DIRECTIONS

1. Measure depth (d) and width (w) of purse. Place fabric flat on table and mark on it a rectangle measuring the width of the purse by twice the depth of the purse. At the center of each side of the rectangle, measure 1 inch beyond rectangle. Draw an oval connecting corners of rectangle to these 1-inch extensions, as shown in *Diagram 6-K1.* Cut out on lines of oval.

2. Glue or sew ball fringe completely around the outer edge of the oval. Place fringe so that it hangs out from fabric, not in toward the center. If glued, let dry completely.

3. Slash an opening in the center of the oval, measuring the exact width of the purse. (See *Diagram 6-K1.*)

4. Turn raw edge of fabric of this slash under ¼ inch and glue to wrong side to secure. Let dry completely.

5. Place fabric over purse, aligning opening with the edge of the top zipper opening. (Wrong side of fabric touches purse.) Glue fabric cover to purse around the top.

Rejuvenated Hat

DIAGRAM 6-LL

Here's a quick and inexpensive way to renew a worn pillbox hat or to make a new but ordinary one look like an original design.

MATERIALS

compass
1 plain pillbox hat of straw or felt
1 felt rectangle, 9 by 12 inches, in contrasting color
white resin glue
1 drapery tassel, approximately 2 inches long by 1 inch wide, to match hat

1. Use a compass to draw on the felt rectangle a circle 2 inches smaller than the diameter of the crown of the hat. Mark the exact center of circle lightly with a pencil. Cut out felt circle.

2. Using a ruler and pencil, divide felt circle into halves, then quarters, then eighths. Cut these 8 wedges apart.

3. Place wedges on the crown of the hat ½ inch in from the edge, as shown in illustration, and glue in position. Let dry completely.

4. Use compass to draw on the felt a circle 2 inches in diameter, large enough to just overlap the points of the wedges in the center of the hat. Cut out this circle and glue it in place.

5. Cut a felt strip 10 inches by ½ inch and tie in a bow. Glue bow to the top of the center front of the hat rim.

Glue drapery tassel to hang from center of the bow, making sure it doesn't dangle past the rim bottom, and let dry completely before wearing.

Floppy Knit Hat

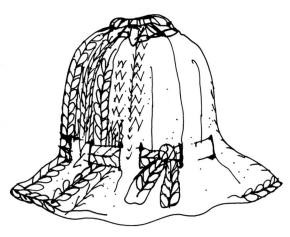

DIAGRAM 6-MM

You can crush and pack this hat, or treat it roughly, and it will always come up looking fresh and perky. It's a cinch to make and will keep your head warm and dry all winter long.

MATERIALS

2 skeins cotton or rayon rug yarn, 1 ounce each, in any desired color
1 pair knitting needles, size #35
1 yarn needle
1 crochet hook, size #K

1. Work with 2 strands of yarn held together throughout. Leaving 18 inches of yarn at beginning of work, cast on 10 stitches. Row 1: * knit 1, increase 1 stitch in the next stitch; repeat from * 4 more times (15 stitches in all).

2. Row 2: Work as for row 1, increasing 7 stitches and ending knit 1 (22 stitches).

3. Row 3: knit across.

4. Row 4: * purl 2, increase 1 stitch in the next stitch; repeat from * 7 more times, ending purl 1 (30 stitches).

5. Rows 5 to 11: Work in stockinette stitch (knit 1 row, purl 1 row) for the next 7 rows. Bind off loosely.

6. Thread yarn needle with 18 inches yarn left in step 1. Sew through the original 10 cast-on stitches and pull up tightly to form a ring. Secure by taking 2 or 3 small stitches in place. Work a loose running stitch to seam sides of hat together. At bottom of seam, work 2 or 3 stitches in place, weave sewing yarn into work for 2 inches, and cut off end.

7. With crochet hook, chain 25 for hatband. End off; cut yarn ends close to beginning and end of chain. Thread hatband through holes in row 8, pull to fit head size, and tie in a knot on the front of the hat.

Felt-brimmed Hat

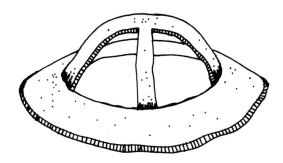

DIAGRAM 6-NN

This easy but fashionable hat can be completed in a matter of minutes to individualize any outfit.

MATERIALS

compass
bonding net, 16 by 16 inches
½ yard felt, in any desired color
white resin glue

1. Use compass to draw 2 circles on felt and 1 on bonding net, each measuring 15¼ inches in diameter. Mark centers of circles lightly with a pencil. Cut out.

2. On each felt circle, center the compass and draw a 6½-inch-diameter circle within, as shown in *Diagram 6-N1*. Cut both out. Do the same with the bonding net circle. Discard centers or reserve for another project.

DIAGRAM 6-N1

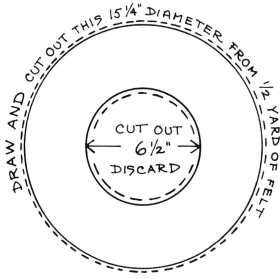

5. With bonding net, attach other felt circle on top.

6. Add a tiny spot of white resin glue to the point at which the strips intersect on the top of the hat, to secure them.

7. If a trim is desired, glue the felt roses or daisies from Chapter 5 to the brim.

DIAGRAM 6-N2

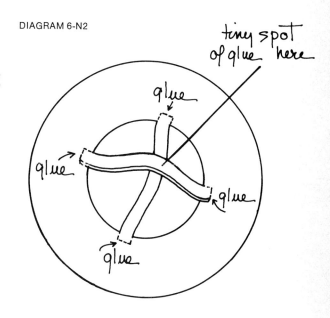

3. Cut 4 felt strips, each measuring 1 by 12 inches. Glue 2 strips together to make 2 double-thickness strips. Let dry completely.

4. Glue ½ inch of each end of these doubled felt strips to opposite sides of 1 felt circle, as shown in *Diagram 6-N2*. Strips will be loopy; they should not lie flat. Let dry.

Rainy Day Hat and Umbrella

DIAGRAM 6-OO

It's amazing what you can do with an inexpensive plastic rain hat from the dime store and a little ingenuity. The matching umbrella completes the ensemble, to turn a rainy day into a sunny one.

The sun motif could also be used on a plastic raincoat.

MATERIALS

2 tubes Glow Writer, 1 yellow and 1 green
brown wrapping paper, 15 by 15 inches
1 white plastic rain hat
1 clear plastic bubble umbrella with yellow or green band

1. *Hat:* Use the sun pattern in *Diagram 6-O1,* or make your own design. Practice writing with

DIAGRAM 6-O1

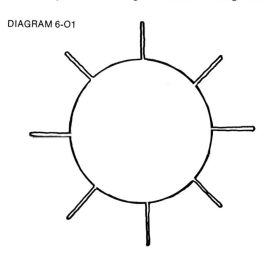

Glow Writer on brown paper to get the feel of it. Determine how large to make your writing so that it fits on the brim of the hat and around the edge of the umbrella.

DIAGRAM 6-O2

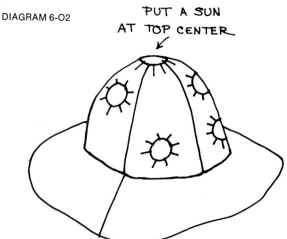

PUT A SUN AT TOP CENTER

2. With yellow Glow Writer draw suns on top sections and in exact top center of hat, as shown in *Diagram 6-O2.*

3. In script, write "Rain, Rain, Go Away— Come Again Another Day" around the brim of the hat, using green Glow Writer. If you have room,

write it twice. Center small dot between phrases.

4. *Umbrella:* Repeat steps 2 and 3 on umbrella, writing verse on the band. Use green Glow Writer on yellow band and yellow Glow Writer on green band.

Monogrammed Stitchery Carrier

DIAGRAM 6-PP

This handy carrier will be an indispensable part of your life if you are a stitchery aficionado. It is designed to open flat, has compartments to prevent yarn and thread from tangling, and, best of all, costs less than $3 to make.

MATERIALS

2 thin flat unfinished wooden suit hangers with rod across the bottom (do not use hangers that curve or are shellacked), ¼ inch thick

1 small can plastic wood

1 sheet medium-grade sandpaper

1 small jar or tube acrylic (or enamel) paint, in any desired color

½ yard felt, in main color

½ yard felt, in contrasting color

white resin glue

20 inches gimp upholstery braid, in main color

3⅛ yards embroidered trim, 2 inches wide, in color to coordinate with both pieces of felt

2 strips nylon fastening tape, each 3 inches long

1. Remove hooks from hangers by twisting the metal out with pliers. Hangers will become bag handles.

2. Fill in hook holes with plastic wood, following directions on can. When dry, sandpaper lightly if necessary.

3. Paint hangers and let dry completely.

4. Cut main color felt into a rectangle 15 by 46 inches. Cut 2 pieces of contrasting color felt, each 12 by 20 inches.

5. Slip the large felt rectangle through both hangers and fold toward center, as shown in *Diagram 6-P1*. This is the inside of the stitchery carrier. Glue ends to center of felt piece to secure; let dry.

6. Completely coat 1 of the smaller felt rectangles with glue. Center it on the inside of the bag, leaving a 1½-inch border all around, and press in place. Let dry.

7. Spread glue on the second small felt rectangle as shown in *Diagram 6-P2*; that is, along both long edges and down centers, both vertical and horizontal, to divide it into 4 pockets. Press in place exactly over same color rectangle. Glue gimp braid lengthwise down the center pocket division.

8. Cut a strip of embroidered trim 15 inches long. Glue this horizontally across the other center pocket division, intersecting the gimp braid and extending past the felt pockets to the outer edge of the bag.

9. Glue remaining embroidered trim along both inside lengthwise edges and both outside lengthwise edges of bag.

10. From remaining main color felt, cut a single pocket 8 by 8 inches for the outside of the bag.

DIAGRAM 6-P1

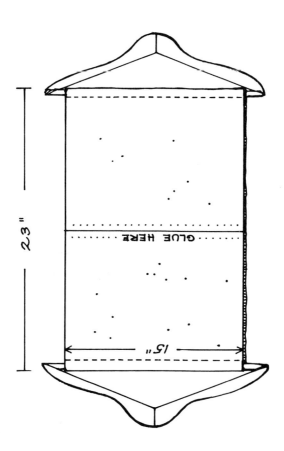

Turn top edge of this piece under 1 inch and glue. Glue along bottom and sides of the pocket and secure it to the center front of the folded bag.

11. Cut your initials from contrasting color felt, and glue on pocket vertically, horizontally, or diagonally, as you prefer. Initials should be about 2 inches high.

12. Glue a strip of nylon fastening tape to the inside center of each side of bag to form a closure next to embroidered trim. (See *Diagram 6- P3.*)

DIAGRAM 6-P2

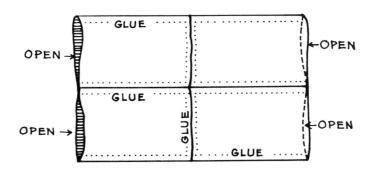

DIAGRAM 6-P3

13. To carry large needlepoint canvases, let rolled canvas extend beyond sides of bag below nylon fastening tape. Yarn and scissors go in pockets. Insert needles in felt anywhere on inside of bag.

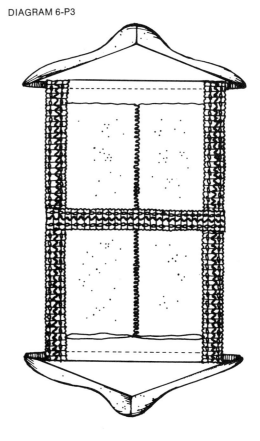

Bicycle-Basket Carryall

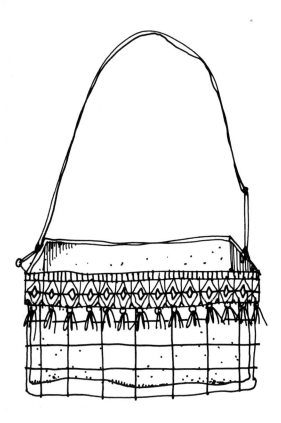

DIAGRAM 6-QQ

This kooky yet practical carryall holds a raft of books or other gear, and will please any teenage girl.

MATERIALS

1 side-type metal bicycle basket with even (not slanted) top
1 can spray paint, in any desired color (optional)
½ yard felt, in any desired color
white resin glue
2 yards (approximately) cotton fringe trim, 3 inches wide, in any desired color
1 leather dog leash, to match, or silver chain-link leash, to match unpainted basket, 3 feet long

1. Spray-paint the bicycle basket if you do not wish to keep the silver metal color.

2. Measure around outside of basket. Measure depth of basket. Cut a felt rectangle to these measurements, adding 5 inches to depth measurement. (See *Diagram 6-Q1.*) This lining will go inside the carryall, and should be long enough to cover all 4 sides and the bottom.

DIAGRAM 6-Q1

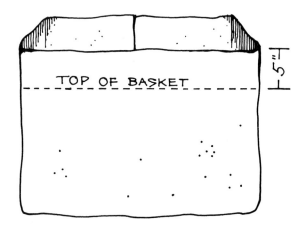

3. Glue the 2 short opposite ends together, overlapping them ¼ inch, as shown in *Diagram 6-Q2.* Let dry.

4. With lining placed before you, as shown in *Diagram 6-Q3,* glue bottom edges together. Let dry completely.

DIAGRAM 6-Q2

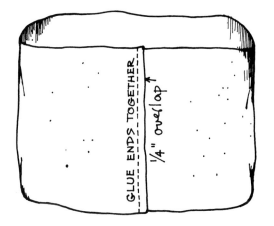

DIAGRAM 6-Q3

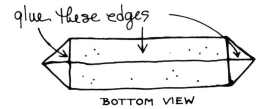

BOTTOM VIEW

5. Turn lining inside out and glue triangular sections at the bottom of each side as shown in *Diagram 6-Q3.* Let dry.

6. Turn lining right side out. Press the glued triangles so that they lie flat. Insert the lining in basket. Glue lining to the top edge of the basket, leaving 1 inch unglued at each top side edge where leash will be attached. Let dry.

7. Glue trim around the outside of the basket at the top, again leaving an opening of 1 inch at each side.

8. Push the loop of the dog leash (the part you hold in your hand) through 1 side of the basket at the top and bring the rest of the leash through this loop to knot it onto that side. Clip the other end of the leash onto the other side of the purse to complete handle, as shown in *Diagram 6-Q4.*

DIAGRAM 6-Q4

7
Children's
Wear

Little Girl's Pinafore

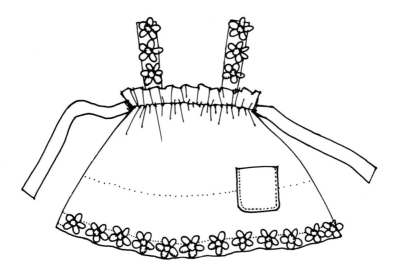

DIAGRAM 7-AA

This design for a party pinafore was inspired by the drawings of Joan Walsh Anglund. I wish I'd been so inspired when my only daughter who's now a teen-ager had been little, for she could have had a whole wardrobe of these enchanting pinafores. Make one for the tiny miss in your family, using a cotton kitchen or bathroom curtain as the base; you'll have it finished in half an hour or less.

MATERIALS

1 cotton kitchen or bathroom cafe-type curtain with a casing (no ruffles or pleats), approximately 25 by 25 inches
1½ yards embroidered washable cotton trim, ¾ inch wide
thread to match curtain or trim

1. Open bottom hem of curtain, using manicure scissors or seam ripper. Pick threads out and press with steam iron.

2. Measure 13 inches from the top edge and cut off. Set bottom part of curtain aside. (See *Diagram 7-A1.*)

3. Turn raw edge (bottom) of top section

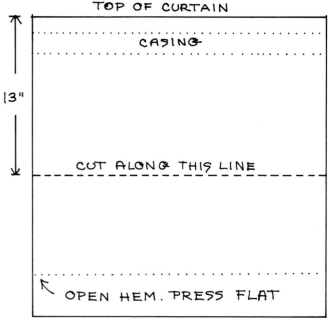

TOP OF CURTAIN

CASING

13"

CUT ALONG THIS LINE

OPEN HEM. PRESS FLAT

DIAGRAM 7-A1

under ¼ inch and press. Now measure a hem of 3 to 5 inches, depending on size of child. Press hem in place; sew by hand or machine. Pin trim along bottom of hem and sew in place.

4. *Sash:* From remaining part of curtain, cut 2 strips, each measuring 2 by 25 inches. Seam edges of these strips together. Fold raw edges (sides and ends) under ¼ inch; press. Stay-stitch in place by hand or machine. The ends of the sash may be tapered by cutting off a triangle. Pull sash through casing of pinafore.

5. *Shoulder straps:* Cut another strip from the remaining fabric, 2½ by 25 inches. Fold in half lengthwise; press. Sew all around ¼ inch from raw edges, leaving a 2-inch opening in center of long side. Using the eraser end of a pencil or the back of a knitting needle, push 1 short closed end of the strap through the fabric to turn it right side out. Press strap. By hand close the 2-inch opening with tiny stitches. Pin trim down center of strap; sew along both edges of trim to secure. Now cut strap into two 12-inch sections. Sew straps to pinafore as shown in *Diagram 7-A2,* placing 1

DIAGRAM 7-A2

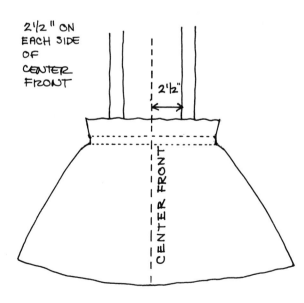

strap 2½ inches on either side of center front. Sew back of straps 1 inch in from outside edge of pinafore.

6. If a pocket is desired, cut from remaining fabric a square 5 by 5 inches. Fold under ¼ inch on 3 sides; press. Fold under ½ inch at top of pocket; press. Sew onto right or left front of pinafore skirt as desired.

Baby's Maxibib

DIAGRAM 7-BB

Terrycloth bibs made from washcloths are a dime a dozen, but this idea features a gay kitchen terrycloth towel that gives extra coverage and can be coordinated to match your kitchen towels. It will protect little clothes for a year or more, even with frequent washing.

MATERIALS

1 terrycloth kitchen towel, in gay motif
1 package cotton twill tape, 1 inch wide, in white
thread in white

1. Cut neckline and shoulder shaping from towel as shown in *Diagram 7-B1*.

2. Fold twill tape in half lengthwise and pin over the diagonal raw edges of the shoulders; sew by hand or machine.

3. Cut 1½ yards of twill tape. Fold in half crosswise and place a pin on fold to mark the center; unfold. Fold bib in half lengthwise and place pin at center of neck; unfold. Fold tape in half lengthwise; match center of tape to center of neckline. Pin folded tape over neckline and sew to cover raw edges. Do not fold or sew end sections of tape, which are the ties.

4. Fold shoulders down 3 inches and with several hand stitches tack in place at the very outer edge to form armholes. (See *Diagram 7-B2*.)

DIAGRAM 7-B1

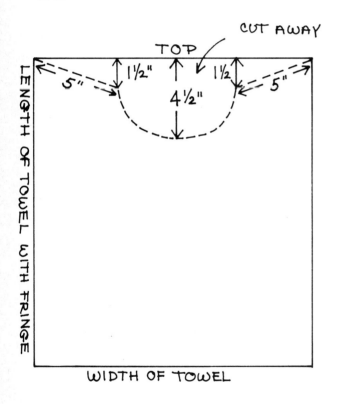

DIAGRAM 7-B2

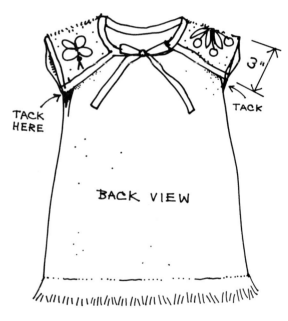

Birthday-Gift Apron

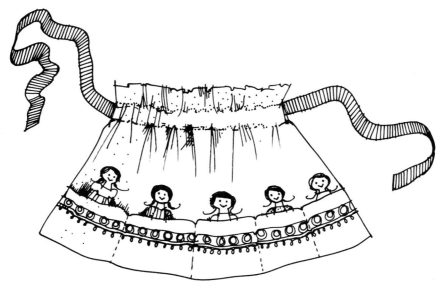

DIAGRAM 7-CC

This little girl's birthday gift can be the hit of any birthday party. Also a most saleable bazaar item, it can be completed in a matter of minutes if you keep a supply of clothespin dolls on hand. (Your children can keep busy making the dolls on rainy days.) Buy the odd-size curtain valances whenever there's a white sale going on.

MATERIALS

1 kitchen or bathroom fabric curtain valance, unruffled, unpleated, and with a casing at the top, approximately 13 by 25 inches, in a solid color

1 yard grosgrain ribbon, 1 inch wide, in contrasting color

thread to match curtain

5 wooden clothespins (not the spring type)

felt-tipped markers, with thin points, in various colors

yarn scraps

5 pipe cleaners

fabric scraps

white resin glue

1. With manicure scissors or a straight pin, open the bottom hem of the curtain; press. Remove all threads from hem. Fold raw edge to *right* side ¼ inch; then fold 3½-inch hem to *right* side. Press. (Do not sew.) Measure the width across bottom and divide by 5. Insert a straight pin vertically through fold to mark each fifth. (For example, if width is 25 inches, place straight pins at 5-inch intervals.) Sew vertically through hem at each pin as shown in *Diagram 7-C1,* to form pockets.

DIAGRAM 7-C1

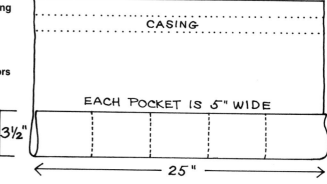

2. Run grosgrain ribbon through the curtain casing at the top for apron ties.

3. *Clothespin dolls:* Draw faces on top part of each clothespin with felt-tipped markers. Cut 2-inch strips of yarn and glue a few of these strips to top of the clothespin for the doll's hair. Tie a pipe cleaner around the clothespin just below the doll's head for arms; bend pipe cleaner to curve the arms slightly. For clothes, cut a 3- by 3-inch square of fabric; gather it along 1 edge. Tie gathered fabric just below the doll's neck and pipe cleaner arms and knot to secure, or tie it at neck over arms, make a tiny slit on each side of dress, and pull arms through. (See *Diagram 7-C2* for completed doll.)

DIAGRAM 7-C2

4. Put 1 doll in each pocket.

Teeny-Weeny Bikini

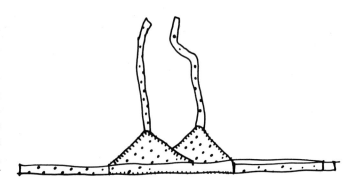

DIAGRAM 7-DD

Made of two washcloths (only one is required for the boy's version), this cunning bikini couldn't be easier to whip up; it will fit a baby weighing up to twenty-five pounds or one year of age. Inexpensive dime-store washcloths are better for this design than luxurious velvety nap ones.

MATERIALS

2 thin matching washcloths, approximately 13 by 13 inches
thread to match

1. *Bikini pants:* Fold 1 washcloth diagonally and cut into 2 triangles. Place triangles 1 on top of another with right sides together.

2. Measure ½ inch up each side from the point of the triangle, and seam triangles together across bottom, as shown in *Diagram 7-D1.*

DIAGRAM 7-D1

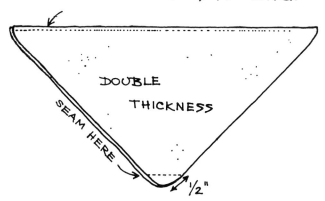

TURN UNDER RAW EDGES ¼". STITCH

DOUBLE

THICKNESS

SEAM HERE

½"

3. Fold raw edge to wrong side ¼ inch; sew. Turn right side out. Knot top corners at sides to secure when wearing.

4. *Bikini halter:* From second washcloth, cut 2 triangles 4 by 4 by 7 inches from opposite corners, as shown in *Diagram 7-D2.*

DIAGRAM 7-D2

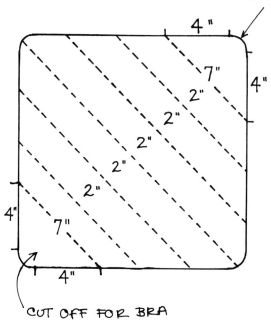

CUT OFF FOR BRA

4"

7"

2"

2"

2"

2"

2"

4"

4"

7"

4"

CUT OFF FOR BRA

5. Cut the remainder of washcloth into at least 5 diagonal strips 2 inches wide.

6. Overlap the 2 triangles as shown in *Diagram 7-D3;* pin together. Pin a 2-inch strip as long as the combined length of bases of both triangles plus a ½-inch extension on each side to base of triangles with right sides facing. Seam together ½ inch from edge. Cut away any excess.

7. Fold band in half lengthwise to wrong side. Pin raw edge of band up to cover raw edges of seam on wrong side.

8. Fold each of the 4 remaining 2-inch-wide strips in half lengthwise; press. Seam along long open edge and 1 short end of each strip.

9. Turn right side out. Press.

10. Pin 1 tie at each side of neck and 1 tie at each side of halter band, with raw edge of tie meeting body of the halter; sew.

DIAGRAM 7-D3

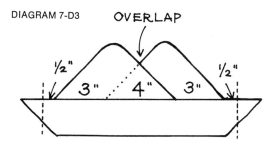

OVERLAP

½"

3"

4"

3"

½"

Old-fashioned Skirt and Stole Ensemble

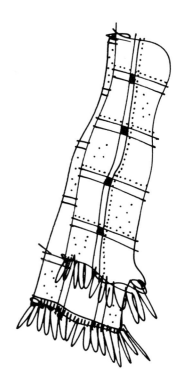

DIAGRAM 7-EE

Fabric left over from a hostess skirt for myself led to this hostess skirt and stole for my teen-age daughter; they took less than an hour to complete. I have also made the same outfit for myself, using hand-embroidered crewel fabric purchased by the yard, without additional trim. The finished skirt cost only $15; similar ones in boutiques sell for $50 or more.

MATERIALS

1 yard bonded knit wool or acrylic fabric, in any desired color
2½ yards cotton fringe trim, 2 inches wide
thread to match fabric
½ yard (approximately) elastic, ½ inch wide

1. *Skirt:* Fold fabric in half lengthwise with right sides together. Measure child to determine width of widest part of hips and length from waist to ankle. Add 5 inches to hip measurement and 1½ inches to length. Cut fabric to desired width and length. Seam the long sides together by hand or machine ½ inch from edge. Press seam open.

2. Fold top edge to wrong side ¼ inch and press. Fold over 1 inch more, press, and stitch along bottom edge to form a casing, leaving 2 inches open to insert elastic.

3. Pull the elastic through casing, overlap it ½ inch, and secure it with a few stitches. Sew casing opening closed.

4. Fold bottom edge of skirt to wrong side for

¼ inch and press. Turn skirt right side out. Pin and sew trim around bottom of skirt.

5. To make a tie belt for the skirt, cut a strip of fabric 3 by 36 inches. Fold all raw edges to wrong side for ¼ inch, press, and stay-stitch. Pin and sew trim to ends. Tie belt over elasticized waistline when wearing.

6. *Stole:* Cut a piece of fabric 15 by 36 inches.

7. Fold all raw edges to wrong side for ¼ inch, press, and stay-stitch.

8. Pin and sew trim along the 2 short ends of the stole.

Converted Snowsuit Jacket

DIAGRAM 7-FF

This thrifty trick quickly converts an outgrown one-piece snowsuit into a child's winter jacket. Putting in a new zipper, using zipper adhesive tape to eliminate basting, is a snap.

MATERIALS

1 infant's or toddler's 1-piece zip-front snowsuit
1 separating zipper to match snowsuit, 10 to 12 inches
zipper adhesive tape (optional)
thread to match snowsuit
1 to 2½ yards embroidered trim, 2½ inches wide, to match or contrast with snowsuit
bonding net (optional)

1. Carefully remove old zipper; cut off bottom of snowsuit all around, 2 to 3 inches below the waistline. (See *Diagram 7-F1.*)

2. Position new zipper, using zipper adhesive tape to hold securely, and sew. Remove tape after stitching.

3. To eliminate a "cut-off" look and to add

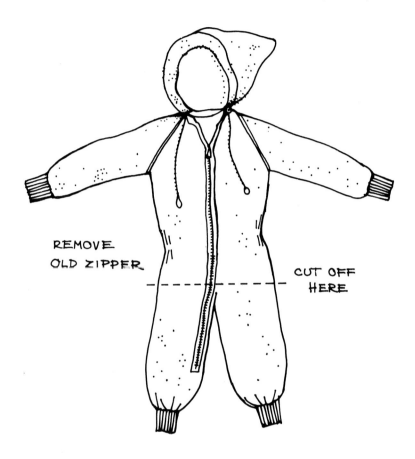

REMOVE
OLD ZIPPER

CUT OFF
HERE

DIAGRAM 7-F1

length to the jacket, pin embroidered trim to the
bottom of the jacket. Apply with bonding net, following package directions, or sew.

4. If desired, bond or sew the same trim to
cuffs, if they are not the knit type. Trim can also
be applied to the edge of the hood or hat.

Little Red Riding Hood Cape

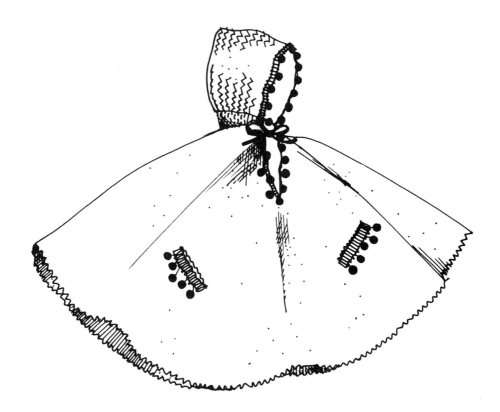

DIAGRAM 7-GG

This is the perfect outfit for an adoring grandma to make for her granddaughter. If you prefer not to knit, you can purchase an inexpensive ready-made knit hood instead and still make this charming hooded cape.

MATERIALS

1½ yards felt, in white or red

1 piece of string, at least 20 inches long

pinking shears (optional)

1½ to 2 yards ball fringe, in red

white resin glue

1 skein 4-ply knitting worsted, 4 ounces

1 pair knitting needles, size #10

1 yarn needle

½ yard grosgrain ribbon, ½ inch wide, in red

1. Measure child from neck to just below the knee to determine length of cape.

2. Fold felt in half and then in quarters. Pin along folded edges to hold. Following directions in Chapter 2 for making a large circle, use string and pencil to draw an arc, the radius of which is the length determined in step 1, onto the top felt quarter.

3. Cut through all 4 layers of felt with pinking shears or straight scissors, following the arc.

4. From same center draw and cut out a small circle, the radius of which is 2½ to 3 inches, for neck opening. Unfold felt circle. Make a 5- to 6-inch slash down the center front of neckline.

5. Measure down 2 or 3 inches directly below this slash and mark with pin. Measure horizontally

DIAGRAM 7-G1

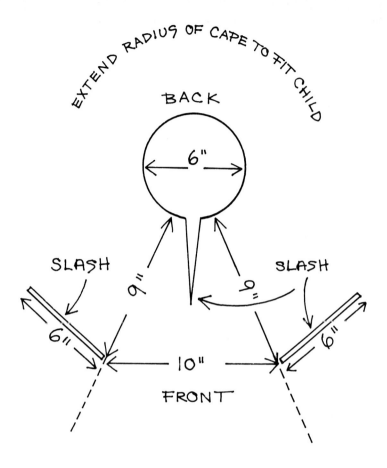

5 inches on each side of center pin marker and mark again for bottom of armholes. From these points, make 2 diagonal slashes for armholes on front of cape, as shown in *Diagram 7-G1*.

6. Glue ball fringe around neck and armhole openings. (Place fringe right at cut edges of felt, except around neck, where it should start ½ inch from cut edge.)

7. *Knit hood:* Cast on 25 stitches and work in stockinette stitch (knit 1 row, purl 1 row) for 12 inches. Bind off loosely. Fold in half crosswise so that both short ends meet, with right (knit) sides facing. Seam along 1 of the long sides, using the same yarn. Weave in ends. Turn hood right side out. Seam is on back of hood.

8. For neckband, cast on 10 stitches and work in garter stitch (knit every row) until piece is as long as bottom of hood. Bind off.

9. With right sides facing, sew the neckband to the hood. Turn right side out.

10. Pin bottom of hood neckband to outside of neck opening of cape, just above ball fringe; sew in place.

11. Cut ribbon in two 9-inch lengths and sew 1 to each side of the hood for ties.

Lion Jumper

DIAGRAM 7-HH

Not only is this cunning jumper easy to make, but it adapts well to any season. For winter, make it in felt, to be worn over tights and a long-sleeved knit top. For summer make it in unbleached muslin or pillow ticking. Most practical for every season is scrubbable vinyl—a quick wipe with a damp cloth and it's as good as new.

MATERIALS

brown wrapping paper, equivalent in size to 2 sheets newspaper
1 yard or more felt, unbleached muslin, or vinyl (1 yard will fit up to size 4)
2 sheets tracing paper
transparent adhesive tape
fabric scraps (for appliqué)
¼ yard bonding net
1 yarn needle

yarn scraps (use felt or washable cottons on muslin and vinyl)
2 black buttons, ½- to ¾-inch diameter
thread to match fabric
white resin glue
1 package rickrack, ¼ inch wide, in any desired color
10 inches cotton or acrylic yarn fringe, 1 inch wide
1 package bias binding (not necessary for vinyl), to match fabric

1. Draw pattern for back of jumper on brown wrapping paper; cut out.

DIAGRAM 7-H1

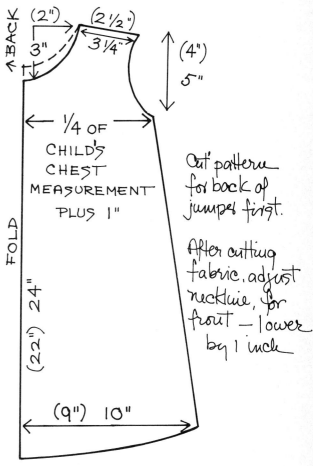

← BACK

(2") 3"

(2½") 3¼"

(4") 5"

← ¼ OF CHILD'S CHEST MEASUREMENT PLUS 1" →

FOLD

(22") 24"

(9") 10"

Cut pattern for back of jumper first.

After cutting fabric, adjust neckline, for front — lower by 1 inch

PATTERN FOR AGE 4-6
BRACKETED NUMBERS — AGE 2-3

DIAGRAM 7-H2

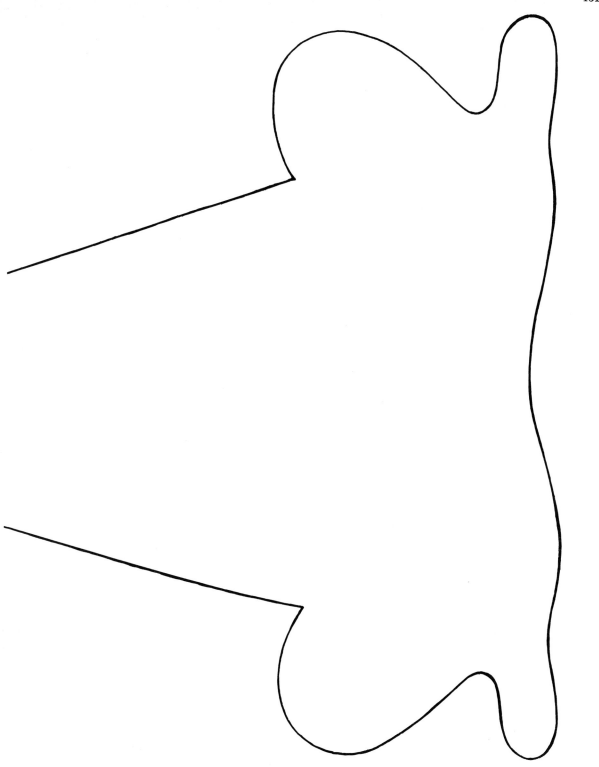

2. Place pattern on fold of fabric; pin. Cut out back of jumper first. Remove pins. Adjust neckline for front of jumper, place on fold of fabric, and pin. Cut out front of jumper. Remove pins. (See *Diagram 7-H1.*)

3. On brown paper, trace and cut out lion appliqué and bow from *Diagram 7-H2,* and pin to fabric scraps. Cut out from the fabric and also cut corresponding pieces from bonding net.

4. With yarn scraps, embroider whiskers, nose, and mouth in satin stitch, as shown in *Diagram 7-H2.*

5. Sew button eyes to lion's head.

6. Align bonding net on jumper front in the desired position. Place lion appliqué over bonding net, and follow package directions to bond. If vinyl appliqué is used, glue to jumper front.

7. Sew or glue 10-inch fringe to top of lion's head.

8. Make lion's tail by sewing rickrack in place (glue to vinyl).

9. Pin jumper front and back together with right sides facing. Sew side and shoulder seams ½ inch from edge. Press seams open.

10. Cover the raw edges of the neck, armholes, and hem with bias binding, following directions on package. For vinyl, turn edges of neck and armholes ¼ inch to wrong side and glue.

All-in-One Jumper

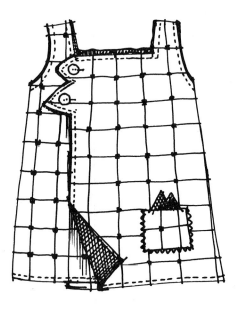

DIAGRAM 7-I1

This is a practical jumper than can be made of felt in a matter of minutes. Or make the lined cotton version: Simply cut out two jumpers in contrasting colors and topstitch them together.

MATERIALS

brown wrapping paper, equivalent in size to 3 sheets newspaper

¾ yard felt, 72 inches wide, or 1 yard fabric (for lined jumper, double quantity of fabric in a contrasting color or pattern), 48 inches wide, in any desired color

thread to match

2 buttons, 1 inch diameter

2 sets large snaps or buttonsnaps

1. Take chest measurement of child. Also measure length from top of shoulder to center of knee. Follow *Diagram 7-I1* and draw pattern for jumper on brown wrapping paper. Cut out pattern.

DIAGRAM 7-I1

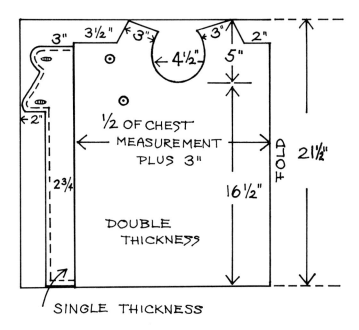

2. Pin pattern to fabric. Cut out. For lined jumper, pin pattern to lining fabric and cut out.

3. Fold each jumper with wrong sides out and sew shoulder seams ½ inch from edges.

4. Fold under ¼ inch all around neck and armhole openings on each jumper piece, hem, and front, and press in place.

5. Carefully pin the 2 jumpers with wrong sides together. Pin at shoulders and all around at 2- or 3-inch intervals. Topstitch together.

6. Cut a square of fabric 5 by 5 inches for a pocket, if desired. Fold under 1 inch on the top and ½ inch on the other 3 sides; press. Pin to jumper and around sides and bottom. Topstitch.

7. Sew 2 buttons in place, as shown in *Diagram 7-I1.* Sew 1 part of a snap directly under each button and the other snap part to the corresponding points on other side of jumper front.

Toddler's Holiday Jumper

DIAGRAM 7-JJ

This jumper doesn't require a single stitch! In red or green, it's a perfect holiday dress-up. To adapt it for any day in the year, see the variation following the design directions. A little girl, or even a large doll, can have a whole wardrobe of these jumpers.

MATERIALS

½ yard felt, in red, green, or any color for all year round

pinking shears (optional)

1 felt rectangle, 9 by 12 inches, in white

compass

1 felt rectangle, 9 by 12 inches, in green or red to contrast with jumper

white resin glue

2 inches fringe, to match large piece of felt (optional)

1 tube multicolor Glitter Magic

1 snap or hook and eye or 1-inch piece of nylon fastening tape

1. Lay fabric out flat.
2. Cut out the jumper, following *Diagram 7-J1,* using pinking shears or regular scissors.
3. Using a compass, draw the snowman on white felt by making one 2¼-inch circle and one 3-inch circle. Cut out.
4. On contrasting felt rectangle, draw hat, mouth, and eyes, plus a ¼- by 4-inch strip for broom handle, as shown in *Diagram 7-J2.* Cut out.
5. Glue snowman in place on center front of jumper. Glue on broom handle. For brush part of broom, glue on fringe (or cut a small piece of felt and slash several times almost to end).
6. With Glitter Magic, write *Merry Christmas* in script all around the bottom and up the back edges of the jumper. Dot felt eyes with Glitter Magic and make Glitter Magic "buttons." Let dry completely.
7. Glue shoulder seams so that the front overlaps the back ¼ inch.
8. Sew snap, hook and eye, or nylon fastening tape to both sides of the back neck opening of the jumper.

Variation: This design features 3 "pop art" flowers in a flowerpot with the child's initials. (See

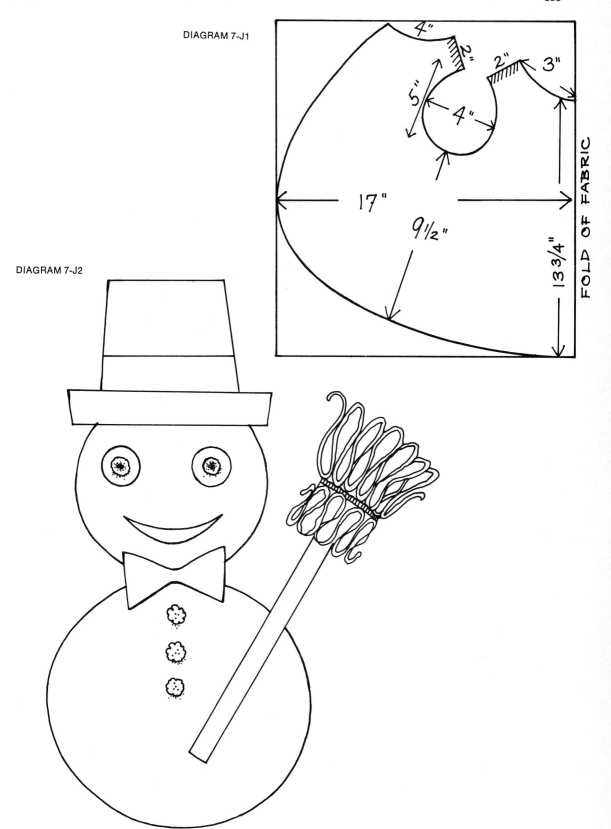

DIAGRAM 7-J1

4"

2"

2" 3"

5"

4"

17"

9½"

13¾"

FOLD OF FABRIC

DIAGRAM 7-J2

156

Diagram 7-J3.) Use any color felt desired, with felt scraps of green and 2 contrasting colors.

1. Cut out the flower shapes from the jumper color and 1 of the contrasting colors as follows: Make three 2-inch circles and three ½-inch circles in first contrasting color and three 1¼-inch circles in jumper color.

2. Cut 3 stems from green felt, each ¼ inch wide by 5 inches long.

3. From second contrasting color felt, cut out a flowerpot. See diagram for dimensions.

4. From the first contrasting color felt, cut a band ½ by 7 inches, for top of the flowerpot. Cut out 1½-inch initials.

5. Assemble as shown and glue in place on the center front of jumper.

6. Finish jumper as described in steps 7 and 8 above.

DIAGRAM 7-J3

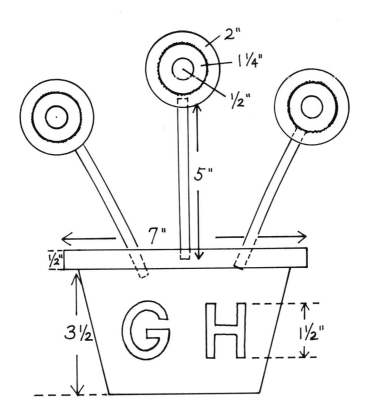

Lacy Party Smock

DIAGRAM 7-KK

Made from lacy plastic place mats costing less than a dollar, this party cover-up can be ready in less than ten minutes. Make it in quantity as a party favor or for bazaars, or make a single one as a special gift for a special little girl.

MATERIALS

2 matching plastic lace place mats (without stiff backing), in white
white resin glue
½ inch nylon fastening tape
2 yards satin ribbon, ½ inch wide, in contrasting color

1. Place mats together, wrong sides facing.
2. From 1 short end of each place mat, cut out neck opening 4 by 1½ inches, as shown in *Diagram 7-K1.*

DIAGRAM 7-K1

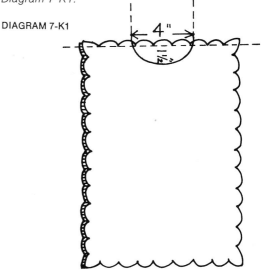

3. Slash 4 inches down the exact center of the back only so that cover-up will slip over child's head. Glue a piece of nylon fastening tape to the top of each side of slash, placing 1 piece of tape on the outside and the other on the inside so that they will lock in place when closed.

4. Lay the 2 place mats out flat, right side up, with neck cutouts touching, as shown in *Diagram 7-K2.*

5. Slide the back shoulder to overlap the front by ¼ inch and glue the shoulder seams together. Let dry completely.

6. Cut ribbon into four 18-inch lengths.

7. Glue 1 length of ribbon to each side of the front and back, 4½ inches down from the shoulder line. Tie at sides.

DIAGRAM 7-K2

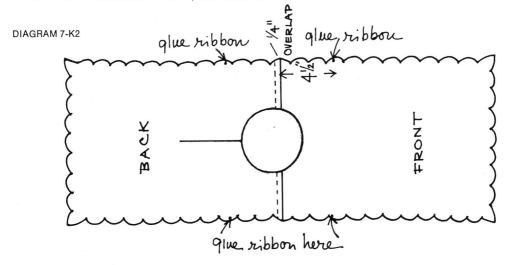

158

Cozy Boot Cuffs

DIAGRAM 7-L1

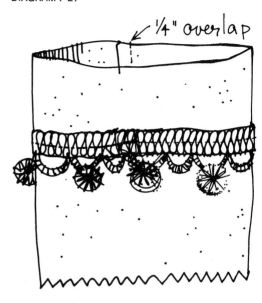

DIAGRAM 7-LL

Here's another good Girl Scout or Brownie project. These boot cuffs have saved many a chapped leg at our house. Children especially love them because they're a project that all but the tiniest children make themselves, at a cost of pennies.

MATERIALS

2 felt rectangles, 9 by 15 inches, both in the same color

30 inches ball fringe or any suitable trim you may have on hand, in contrasting color

white resin glue

1. Bring the 2 short ends of a felt rectangle together to form a cylinder, overlapping ends ¼ inch; glue overlap. (You may need to overlap more to fit the boot-top of a very young child.) Let dry.

2. Turn down 2½ inches at the top on the cylinder to form a cuff.

3. Glue ball fringe to the edge of this cuff as shown in *Diagram 7-L1*. Let dry completely.

4. Repeat with second felt rectangle.

5. To wear, slip the 2½-inch cuff over the top edge of the boot; the deeper part of the cuff stays in the boot to keep the child's leg warm and dry.

Dress-up Hat

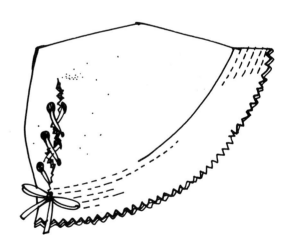

DIAGRAM 7-MM

Here's a smart dress-up hat that can be completed in a half hour or less for girls of all ages. Make it to match a "Sunday-best" ensemble.

MATERIALS

⅓ yard felt, in any desired color
brown wrapping paper
pinking shears (optional)
paper punch
thread to match felt
1 leather thong, in any desired color

1. Cut felt into 4 squares, 12 by 12 inches each; reserve remainder of felt for other projects.

2. On brown wrapping paper, draw hat pattern as shown in *Diagram 7-M1.* Cut out. Pin to each square of felt in turn; trace around and cut out with pinking shears.

3. On each piece of felt, make 4 holes on each straight side edge, as shown in *Diagram 7-M2,* using a paper punch.

4. Stack all 4 pieces together (for extra body and warmth in the hat) and pin to hold securely. Topstitch through all 4 layers along the edge of the brim, starting at the very center edge. Work 7 or 8 rows of topstitching at ⅛-inch intervals to make the brim quite stiff.

5. Cut leather thong in half. Lace each side of the hat from top to bottom, the way you lace shoes, and end with a bow as shown in *Diagram 7-M3.* Cut away any thong not needed for the bow.

DIAGRAM 7-M2

DIAGRAM 7-M3

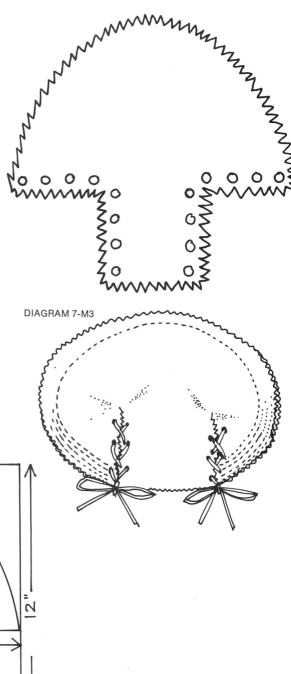

DIAGRAM 7-M1

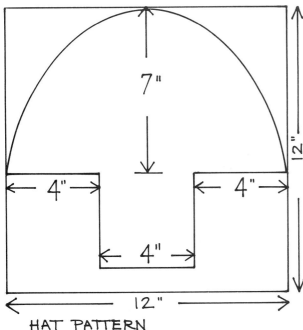

HAT PATTERN

Mary Poppins Hat

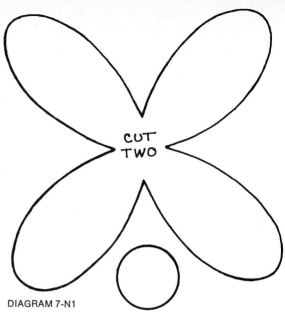

DIAGRAM 7-N1

DIAGRAM 7-NN

This perky stand-up flower looks well on a Sunday hat; it is equally effective on a plain white sailor's hat, the kind sold at the dime store during the summer for wearing at the beach. Girls of about ten years or older might enjoy making this project themselves.

MATERIALS

⅛ yard felt, in green
1 sheet tracing paper
1 felt rectangle, 9 by 12 inches, in any desired color
white resin glue
1 inexpensive ready-made hat with brim
1 pipe cleaner, in green (if you can't find a green one, color a white pipe cleaner with a green felt-tipped marker)

1. From green felt, cut a strip 1 inch wide and 55 inches long for hatband.

2. Trace the flower in *Diagram 7-N1;* cut out. Pin to contrasting felt rectangle and cut out. Repeat so that you have 2 pattern pieces. Trace and cut out leaves from green felt, following *Diagram 7-N2.*

3. Glue hatband into position on crown of hat so that center of felt strip is at center front of hat. Tie a bow and let long ends hang down in back.

4. Align the 2 sets of petals on top of each other and then move the top cutout so that its petals fit between the bottom ones. Glue together at the very center.

5. Trace around a nickel onto green felt and cut out for center of flower. Glue green center to the center of the petals already joined together.

6. Glue completed flower (at the center back) to top of pipe cleaner. Slip bottom of pipe cleaner under hatband so that 2 inches extend beneath it. Glue leaves in place on brim. Curl bottom end of pipe cleaner stem upwards.

DIAGRAM 7-N2

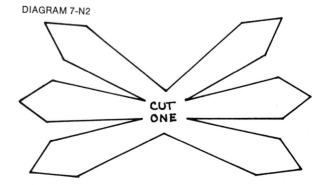

Bug Belt

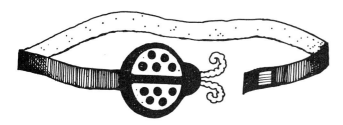

DIAGRAM 7-OO

This felt belt for boys or girls can be completed in about an hour and a half. The directions are for making fifteen belts; the materials will cost about 30 cents per belt—all of which makes this a perfect project for Scout troops or after-school crafts clubs.

MATERIALS

1¼ yards felt (each belt requires a strip 3 inches wide and as long as the child's waist measurement plus 2 inches), in any desired color
felt scrap, 3 by 3 inches, in contrasting color
white resin glue
tracing paper
3 pieces shirt cardboard, 9 by 12 inches, or 1 sheet poster board
3 to 4 felt rectangles, 9 by 15 inches, in assorted colors
paper punch (optional)
6 pipe cleaners
1 small jar acrylic paint, in black
1 small paintbrush
½ yard nylon fastening tape, cut into 1-inch pieces

1. Cut felt into strips 3 inches wide and about 32 inches long. (This may be done in advance by an adult.)

2. Cut off 1 end of strip as many inches as necessary to fit child's waist measurement plus 2 inches. (This and the following steps may be done by children.)

3. Fold strip lengthwise into equal thirds; glue to secure.

4. Trace pattern from *Diagram 7-O1;* cut out.

DIAGRAM 7-O1

5. Paste bug pattern on cardboard and cut out a cardboard bug. Trace around the cardboard bug twice more on cardboard and cut out. There should be 3 cardboard bugs for each belt.

6. Use 1 cardboard bug as a pattern, and trace around it on contrasting color felt. Cut out 1 felt bug.

7. Glue the 3 cardboard bugs together to make 1 thick bug. Glue the felt bug on the top of the cardboard one. Cut out bug's wings from contrasting color felt. If desired, punch out spots in bug's wings with paper punch and glue wings onto body.

8. Cut pipe cleaners into 1-inch lengths. Take 2 of these for each bug, and curl slightly. Glue to top center of bug's head for antennae.

9. Paint the outer cardboard edges black. Also paint the antennae black. Be careful not to paint the felt. This will become the buckle.

10. Glue the unpainted cardboard part of the

bug buckle to 1 end of the long felt strip. (See *Diagram 7-O2.*)

DIAGRAM 7-O2

11. Glue 1 part of nylon fastening tape to the underside of the buckle and another part to the corresponding point on the right (top) side of the other end of belt. (See *Diagram 7-O2.*)

Paper Punch Felt Belt

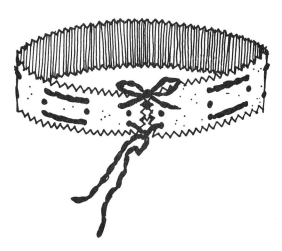

DIAGRAM 7-PP

This gay cummerbund belt is another good group project, easy enough for even eight-year-olds to make. Instructions are for making one belt.

MATERIALS

⅛ yard approximately felt (amount needed is 3 inches wide and as long as required waist measurement), in each of 2 colors
pinking shears (optional)
paper punch
2½ yards decorative yarn gift tie
white resin glue

1. With pinking shears or regular scissors, cut 1 piece of each color felt 3 inches wide and as long as required waist measurement.
2. Punch 3 rows of holes in 1 felt strip, leaving ½ inch between rows and making holes 2 inches apart on each row, as shown in *Diagram 7-P1.* Do not punch holes in the other felt strip.

DIAGRAM 7-P1

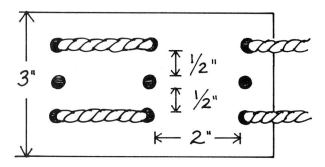

3. Cut yarn exactly in half. Weave 1 yarn piece through the top row of holes and the other through the bottom row. Do not weave through center row of holes.
4. Glue second felt strip to the back of the first felt strip. Let dry completely.
5. To wear, tie yarn in 2 bows at waist.

Heirloom Baby Bonnet

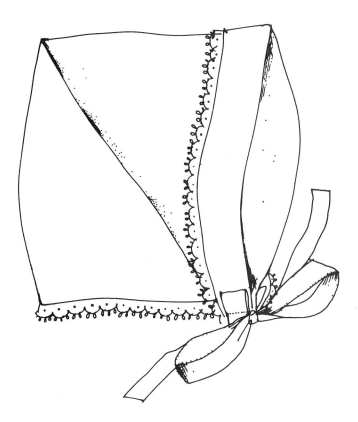

DIAGRAM 7-QQ

This pretty bonnet for a newborn to wear, possibly at the christening, is almost certain to become an heirloom. Made from a handkerchief, it may easily, with a few snips of thread, become a handkerchief again, to be carried by the bride on the "baby's" wedding day.

MATERIALS

1 lace-edged handkerchief, approximately 12 by 12 inches, in white
thread in white
18 inches satin ribbon, ½ inch wide, in white

1. Fold 1 side of handkerchief as shown in *Diagram 7-Q1.* Leave a margin of 1½ inches single thickness at 1 side. Measure, and mark center of folded edge with a pin. Measure 2 inches on each side of center and mark with pins (points B in *Diagram 7-Q1*). Do not stitch.

2. Sew diagonals AB with loose running stitches, making stitches about ¼ inch long. This forms crown of hat, which is now inside out.

3. Fold the unfolded single edge of handkerchief back over doubled portion, making fold 1 inch from edge, as shown in *Diagram 7-Q1.* Press.

DIAGRAM 7-Q1

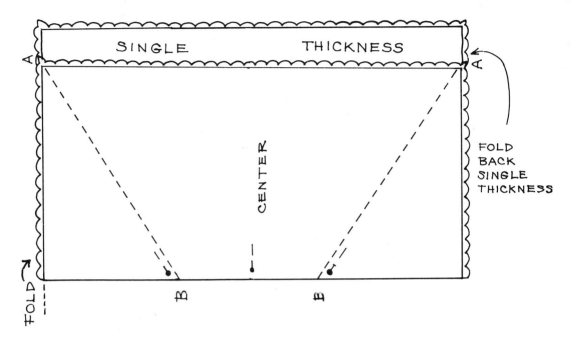

4. Cut ribbon into two 9-inch lengths. Fold under 1 end of each for ½ inch. Sew folded end of ribbon to corner of brim. (See *Diagram 7-QQ.*) Cut other end of each tie on a diagonal.

5. Turn the crown portion of hat right side out so that doubled "triangles" are on inside. Brim remains as pressed.

"Embroidered" Belt

DIAGRAM 7-RR

Here's a quickie belt with a "now" look, easy enough for young girls to make.

MATERIALS

1 yard embroidered cotton ribbon, 2 inches wide
felt, 2¼ by 54 inches, in any desired color
white resin glue

1. Measure around hips, and cut embroidered ribbon 3 inches longer than hip measurement.

2. Fold the felt strip exactly in half, bringing the 2 short ends together. Place a pin on fold as a marker. Unfold. Repeat for ribbon.

3. Match up pin markers, and pin felt and ribbon together with wrong side of trim facing felt. Leave a ⅛-inch border of felt on top and bottom of ribbon. Fold each short end of ribbon under ¼ inch to conceal raw edges. Glue ribbon to felt; remove pins. Let dry completely.

4. With pencil and ruler, draw 5 lines ⅜ inch apart on each end of felt, extending from end of ribbon to end of felt. Cut on each ruled line to make a felt fringe. (See *Diagram 7-R1.*) There should be 6 strips at each end.

5. Knot ends of belt above fringe to wear.

DIAGRAM 7-R1

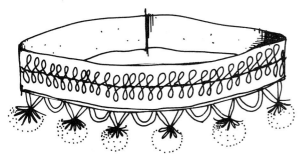

Fancy Fringed Necklace

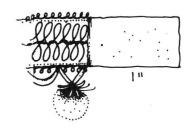

DIAGRAM 7-SS

Here's a fun craft project that even a very young girl can do. Scissors and glue are the only tools required. You'll probably have the felt scraps and *trim on hand; but if you don't, your investment won't be more than 25 cents. Mothers should note the variation using beautiful drapery trim to make an elegant adult version.*

MATERIALS

1 felt strip (length determined by the neck measurement plus 1 inch), ½ inch wide, in any desired color

ball fringe (length determined by exact neck measurement), in any desired color

white resin glue

½ inch nylon fastening tape or hook and eye

thread to match felt

1. Glue ball fringe on felt strip, starting 1 inch from 1 end of felt. (See *Diagram 7-S1.*)

DIAGRAM 7-S1

2. Cut nylon fastening tape in half. Glue 1 piece to the outside of this 1 inch of felt and the other underneath the opposite end of the necklace, or sew a hook and eye to ends for closure.

Variation: Buy the most luxurious silk drapery fringe you can find. Some of these fringes cost as much as $10 a yard, but since you'll need only as much as your neck measurement, your investment will be less than half that price. Some imported fringes come with silk-wrapped wooden tassels. Follow steps 1 and 2 of the child's pattern, using silk drapery fringe instead of ball fringe.

Jumbo Knit Bag

DIAGRAM 7-TT

This perky shoulder bag should delight any young miss. It was made in Fourth-of-July colors, but it can be made in any three-color combination.

MATERIALS

3 skeins 4-ply knitting worsted, 2 ounces each, in red, white, and blue

1 pair knitting needles, size #35

1 yarn needle

1 crochet hook, size #K

1. Working with 3 strands of yarn held together throughout, cast on 15 stitches.

    2. Rows 1 to 5: knit 5, purl 5, knit 5.

    3. Rows 6 to 10: purl 5, knit 5, purl 5.

    4. Rows 11 to 15: repeat rows 1 to 5.

    5. Rows 16 to 20: repeat rows 6 to 10.

    6. Bind off loosely, leaving 2 yards of each strand of yarn to make handle.

    7. Fold work in half with right sides out, bringing the bound-off row up to the beginning row. Thread needle with 1 strand of yarn and seam both sides. Work loose overcast stitches on outside of purse.

    8. For the handle of the purse, pick up 3 strands of a stitch at the top side seam of the purse (where lengths of yarn are still attached) with crochet hook. Chain for 16 inches and secure the last chain to the top of the other side seam with a slip stitch. Chain 1, turn, and single crochet in every chain stitch across handle. Slip stitch into stitch you picked up to start chain, pull yarn through, and weave the last few inches of yarn into the side of the purse. Cut away any excess yarn.

Dolly Purse

DIAGRAM 7-UU

Four little nieces under four years of age were the inspiration for this cunning doll-face purse. It was a bigger hit than any toy I could have bought for them. For a special treat, when giving the purse as a gift, I fill it with play make-up, comb, brush, and a mirror.

MATERIALS

compass
1 inexpensive child's flat-sided round plastic purse, approximately 7-inch diameter
1 felt rectangle, 9 by 12 inches, in yellow, brown, or black (to match the child's hair color)
scraps of felt, in red and black
white resin glue

1. For doll's hair, use compass to draw a circle on the felt rectangle the diameter of the purse. Cut out.

2. Trim circle as shown in *Diagram 7-U1.*

DIAGRAM 7-U1

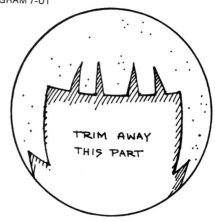

TRIM AWAY THIS PART

3. Using a nickel as a guide, trace and cut out 2 black felt eyes; also cut out a small black felt triangle for the nose.

4. Draw a circle 2½ inches in diameter on red felt. Cut out and trim away ⅔ of the circle for a smiling mouth, as shown in *Diagram 7-U2*.

5. Glue hair, eyes, nose, and mouth in place on purse, as shown on sketch of project; let dry.

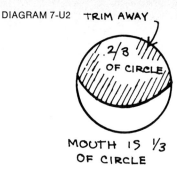

DIAGRAM 7-U2 TRIM AWAY

⅔ OF CIRCLE

MOUTH IS ⅓ OF CIRCLE

Monogrammed Felt Handbag

DIAGRAM 7-VV

Girls of about ten years or older should be able to make this purse without a grownup's help. Although the version illustrated is stitched by machine, it can as easily be glued together. Instead of using felt initials to trim the purse flap, you might add the felt toggle button or the felt flowers from Chapter 5.

MATERIALS

brown wrapping paper
2 felt rectangles, 12 by 15 inches, in any desired color
1 felt rectangle, 9 by 12 inches, in contrasting color
thread to match larger felt pieces or white resin glue
4 brass paper fasteners
1 inch nylon fastening tape

1. Draw pattern for body of purse on brown paper, following *Diagram 7-V1*. Cut out. Place the larger 2 felt rectangles exactly on top of each other. Pin pattern to the double-thick rectangle and cut 2 felt purse bodies. These 2 purse bodies will become the double-thick back and front flap of the purse.

2. Draw pattern for front of purse on brown paper, as shown in *Diagram 7-V2;* cut out. Pin to contrasting color felt and cut 1 piece. This piece will become the single-fold purse front to be over-lapped by the front flap.

3. From the main color felt, cut a felt strip for purse handle 2 by 15 inches. Fold in half length-wise; press. Glue or topstitch the long edge to secure. If glued, let dry completely.

4. Place the 2 identical purse body pieces directly together. Position the single-fold, con-trasting color purse front directly over bottom part of double-thickness purse body. Sew completely

DIAGRAM 7-V1

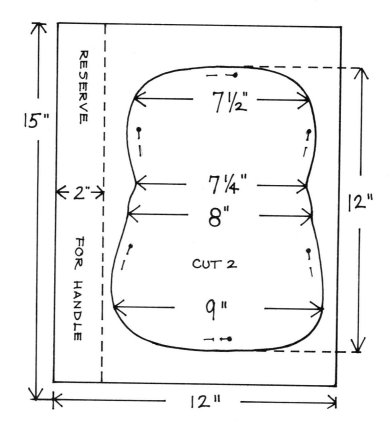

around all outer edges (topstitch by machine ⅛ inch from edge). See *Diagram 7-V3*. Pieces may also be glued together; if so, let dry completely.

5. Attach handle to the top sides of the purse in back of flap at point of fold, using 2 brass paper fasteners to secure each end. The prong part of fasteners should be on the inside of the flap.

6. Sew or glue ½ of the nylon fastening tape to the center inside of the flap and the other ½ to the corresponding point on the outside of the purse front.

7. Cut out initials from the contrasting color felt and glue in the outside center of the flap; or trim as desired.

DIAGRAM 7-V2

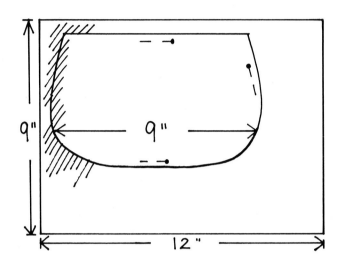

DIAGRAM 7-V3

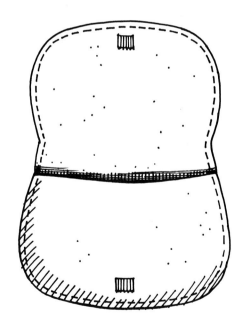

Ribboned Pocketbook

DIAGRAM 7-WW

Using a lattice-type plastic basket of the sort that strawberries and cherry tomatoes come in, any young girl will love making this adorable purse for herself, her sister, or a friend.

MATERIALS

1 piece cardboard
1 plastic berry basket, 1-pint size
felt scraps
2 yards rayon seam binding, in any desired color
10 inches decorative gift-tie yarn, in any desired color

1. Place basket upside down on cardboard and trace around it. Cut out cardboard to make a lid for top of basket.

DIAGRAM 7-W1

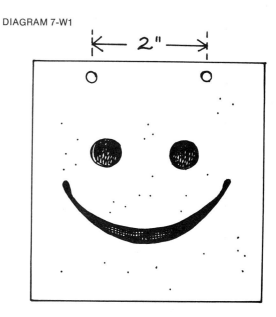

2. Cut 2 pieces of felt the same size as the cardboard. Glue each felt piece to 1 side of cardboard. Let dry.

3. Cut seam binding into 18-inch strips, and reserve 1 strip for step 7.

4. Weave 1 strip of seam binding through the lattice on the top row of the basket. Repeat for the second and third rows. Glue seam binding at the end of each row to secure it. Cut away excess.

5. Cut eyes and mouth out of felt scraps and glue to lid as shown in *Diagram 7-W1;* or trim as desired.

6. Make 2 holes about 2 inches apart on 1 side of the lid of the purse, as shown in *Diagram 7-W1.*

7. Cut two 4-inch pieces of seam binding. Put 1 through each hole and tie through the top row of lattice holes, knotting to secure the lid to the basket. The purse opens from the front. Cut away excess seam binding.

8. Attach yarn handle by knotting at each side of basket through the top row of lattice.

Margarine-Container Purse

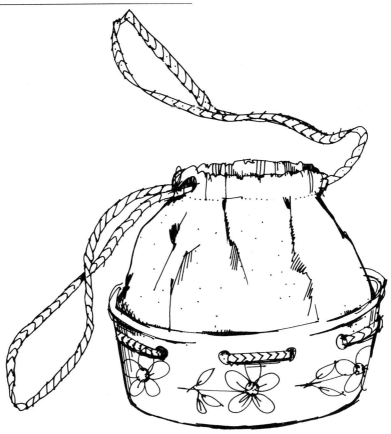

DIAGRAM 7-XX

Any tiny girl will adore this little purse. Perhaps an older sister can make it for her. It costs but pennies to make and will give hours of pleasure to the small recipient. For extra fun, tuck some play money from the dime store inside.

MATERIALS

1 felt rectangle, 9 by 12 inches, in any desired color
white resin glue
1 decorative round plastic margarine container (sides
may be straight or slanted), 4-inch diameter, 2
inches deep
paper punch
2 yards gift-tie cord, in gold

1. Trim 2 inches off one 9-inch side of the felt

DIAGRAM 7-X1

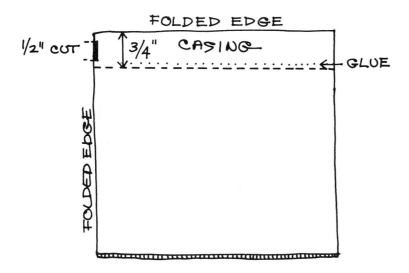

rectangle and set aside for other projects. The felt now measures 7 by 12 inches.

2. Fold 1 long side of felt under ¾ inch, and carefully glue just along the edge to secure. This forms a casing for the drawstring; do not place glue on entire width of flap. Cover with waxed paper or aluminum foil. Weight with a book until completely dry.

3. Fold piece in half crosswise; cut through center of casing ½ inch to make second opening for drawstring. (See *Diagram 7-X1.*)

4. Fit the felt piece around the outside of the plastic container with the casing at the top to determine the fit. Add ¼ inch and cut felt to this measure. (The felt will go inside the purse, but it's easier to measure on the outside.)

5. Now place felt inside the container with casing at the top. Overlap the ends ¼ inch; if necessary, trim away any excess. Glue ¼-inch seam to form a cylinder, leaving the casing part (the top ¾ inch) unglued. (See *Diagram 7-X2.*)

6. With a paper punch, punch holes around

the top edge of the container at 1-inch intervals. Holes should be ¼ inch from top edge. Punch holes also at 1-inch intervals around the bottom of the felt cylinder to correspond to the holes in the container. (See *Diagram 7-X3.*)

DIAGRAM 7-X2

DIAGRAM 7-X3

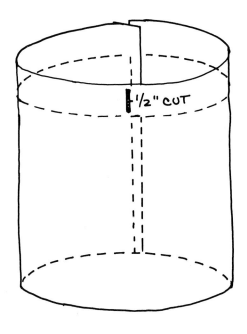

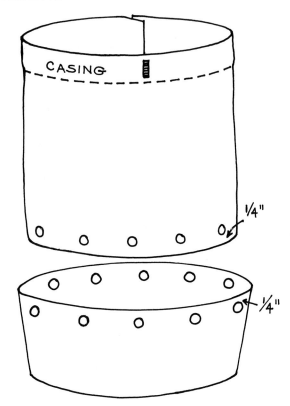

7. Lace the 2 pieces (the felt and the container) together with a 15-inch piece of gold cord gift wrap tie. (See *Diagram 7-X4.*) Tie a knot to secure and cut the ends very short. Push these short ends to the inside of the purse.

8. Fold the remaining gold cord in half and knot ends together. Use a small safety pin to push the doubled cord through the casing, coming out through same opening.

9. Cut off knot. Also cut cord at center (where you folded it). You now have 2 cords in the casing. Knot both ends of each cord together. (See *Diagram 7-X5.*) Cut off any excess cord. Pull 1 looped cord through each opening in casing to form drawstrings.

DIAGRAM 7-X4

DIAGRAM 7-X5

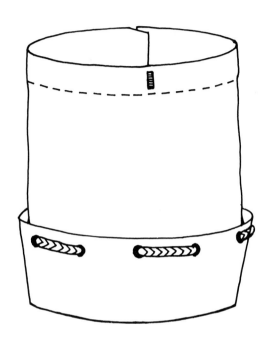

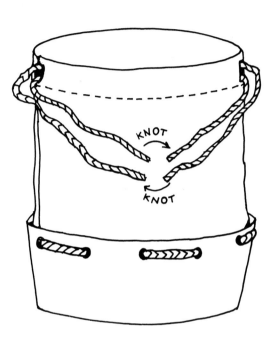

8
Fashions
for Men
and Boys

Detective-Story Shorts and T-Shirt Set

DIAGRAM 8-AA

During a visit to the FBI headquarters in Washington, D.C., my two small boys became so intrigued with the Fingerprint Division that I thought up this idea for them. A word of caution: It's best if the children do this project outdoors in the driveway or on a sidewalk; have a bucket of water and some rags handy! Note the variation at the end.

MATERIALS

1 pair worn cotton slacks (with torn knees) or inexpensive shorts, in light color
newspaper
1 small jar acrylic or textile paint, in black or any dark color
1 paintbrush, 1 inch wide
bucket of water or garden hose
rags
1 inexpensive cotton knit T-shirt, in white or light color

1. Cut pants legs off 4 to 5 inches above knee. Discard worn parts.

2. With a straight pin or a 1-inch brad (nail), make ½-inch fringe all around the edges of the cut-off pants.

3. Place several sheets of newspaper on the ground. Place some newspaper inside shorts and put shorts on the newspaper-covered ground.

4. Wash and dry child's foot (either right or left). Dip brush in black paint. (You may have to dilute paint with water slightly—it shouldn't be too gummy). Brush paint on bottom of child's foot.

5. Let child place foot on shorts. Be sure to have child press down on toes for a complete print. Child should make footprints all over 1 side of shorts. Recoat foot with paint for each print. To print other side of shorts, turn them over. Paint will not smear noticeably.

6. Hang shorts on clothesline until completely dry. Wash child's foot with rags and water. A bar of soap is useful, but the acrylic paint will come off easily with just water if washing is done immediately.

7. Repeat process for T-shirt, using handprints. When finished, wash paintbrush and let dry hanging or flat.

Variation: This project can also be done in reverse, using blue jeans, a dark T-shirt, and white acrylic or textile paint.

Barbecue Chef Apron

1. Fold fabric in half lengthwise.

2. Enlarge apron pattern on brown wrapping paper, following *Diagram 8-B1.* Cut out.

3. Tape pattern to fabric. Cut out the apron.

4. If a pocket is desired, glue the vinyl piece cut out from the neck to the apron, as shown in *Diagram 8-B1.*

DIAGRAM 8-B1

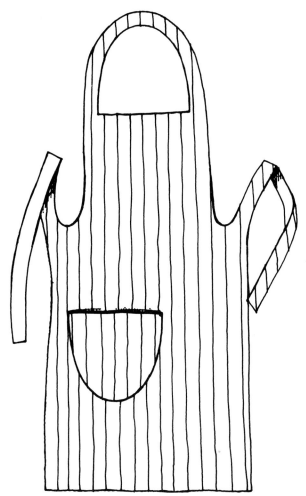

DIAGRAM 8-BB

This handy coverall is a perfect barbecue or work apron for the men of the family, and you'll find it a practical cover-up for you to wear for your craft projects, too. One size fits all, and, best of all, all you do is cut it out! There's no sewing, no gluing, no bonding.

MATERIALS

1½ yards vinyl, not fabric-backed

brown wrapping paper, equivalent in size to 4 sheets newspaper

masking or transparent tape

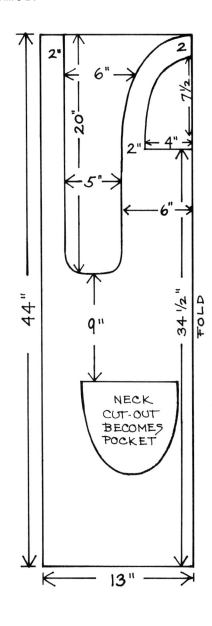

Tuxedo Apron

DIAGRAM 8-CC

The idea for this apron came from my husband, but the design is mine. It's a handsome and practical bar apron that can be made in less than forty-five minutes.

MATERIALS

1 yard fabric-backed vinyl, in black
brown wrapping paper
masking or transparent adhesive tape
½ yard fabric-backed vinyl, in white
white resin glue
tracing paper
4 flat rhinestone buttons, ¼- to ½-inch diameter
1½ yards grosgrain ribbon, 1 inch wide, in black

1. Fold the black vinyl in half lengthwise.
2. On brown paper, enlarge the pattern

shown in *Diagram 8-C1.* Cut out. Tape pattern on black vinyl and cut out.

DIAGRAM 8-C1

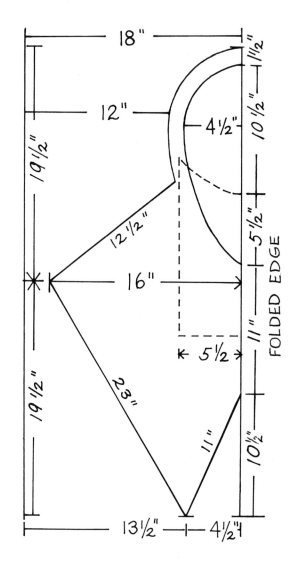

3. Draw neckline insert from *Diagram 8-C2* on brown paper; cut out. Tape to white vinyl and cut out.
4. Glue the white neckline insert under the edges of the neckline cutout on the black bib of the apron.
5. Trace bow tie from *Diagram 8-C3;* cut out.

Tape to black vinyl and cut out. Glue in place at top of white neck insert.

    6. Glue or sew the buttons on the white insert in a straight line below the tie.

    7. Glue a 27-inch length of ribbon to each side of the waist for ties. Let dry completely.

DIAGRAM 8-C2

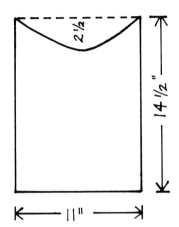

DIAGRAM 8-C3

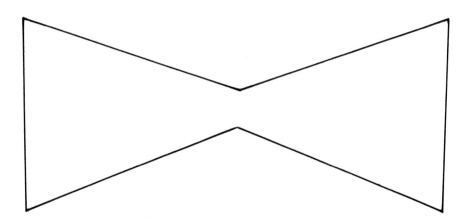

Checkerboard Bargello Belt

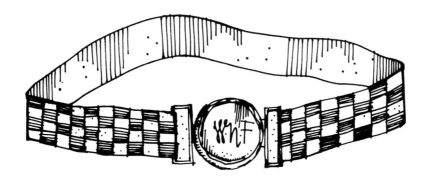

DIAGRAM 8-DD

This belt is practically foolproof to make for even a needlework novice. My teen-age daughter completed it in about three evenings. If you need help with bargello, read the basic bargello instructions in Chapter 2.

MATERIALS

masking tape, 1 inch wide

canvas mesh (length determined by waist measurement), 4 inches wide, size #12

30 strands (approximately) Persian yarn, in any desired color

30 strands (approximately) Persian yarn, in contrasting color

1 tapestry or needlepoint needle

white resin glue

grosgrain ribbon (length determined by waist measurement), 1 or 1¼ inches wide, in 1 of yarn colors

1 link-type belt buckle

1. Cut 4 pieces of masking tape to fit each side of canvas. Tape canvas on all sides, folding tape over edge of canvas to bind it.

2. Pattern is a checkerboard worked in alter-nate groups of 4 stitches. Each stitch is worked vertically over 4 meshes of canvas. (See *Diagram 8-D1.*) Work in pattern until the desired length is reached (waist measurement minus 1 inch).

3. Trim canvas to within ½ inch of the stitchery on all sides. With steam iron and damp cloth, press this ½ inch to the wrong side of work *on long sides only.*

4. Spread glue on grosgrain ribbon to within

DIAGRAM 8-D1

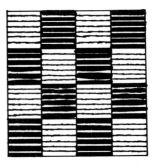

1 inch of each end. Center on wrong side of work, covering the folded ½-inch margins. Do not glue the ends of the ribbon; leave loose for step 6.

5. Protect with aluminum foil or waxed paper; top with heavy books. Let dry completely.

6. Insert each end of belt through a section of the belt buckle. (See *Diagram 8-D2.*) Adjust to waist size if necessary. There should be ¼ inch of stitching and ½ inch of raw canvas margin on wrong side. Glue to secure. Fold end of ribbon under to fit and glue to cover raw canvas. Protect and press under heavy books until dry, as before.

DIAGRAM 8-D2

PUSH EACH END OF BELT THROUGH SLOT OF CORRESPONDING BUCKLE AND GLUE

Diamond-Pattern Bargello Belt

DIAGRAM 8-EE

There are few things I love to do more than bargello! Ever since I learned how to do it, I have been addicted, traveling around with canvas, needle, and Persian yarn. Since my house already has too many pillows, I have had to invent other uses for my huge bargello output. This is one of them. If you're a novice, read the basic bargello instructions in Chapter 2, and try the beginner's belt pattern, in this chapter, before attempting this one.

MATERIALS

masking tape, 1 inch wide
canvas mesh (length determined by waist measure-
    ment plus 8 inches), 4 inches wide, size #12
1 tapestry or needlepoint needle
30 strands Persian yarn, in main color
30 strands Persian yarn, in contrasting color
30 strands Persian yarn, in second contrasting color
grosgrain ribbon (length the same as that of canvas
    mesh), 2 inches wide
white resin glue
1 belt buckle with a 2-inch buckle rod

1. Cut 4 pieces of masking tape to fit each side of canvas. Bind raw edges of canvas on all 4 sides, folding tape over edges to prevent raveling.

2. Study *Diagram 8-E1;* make the diamond outlines first, using the first contrasting color yarn. Each stitch is worked vertically over 4 squares of the canvas mesh.

DIAGRAM 8-E1

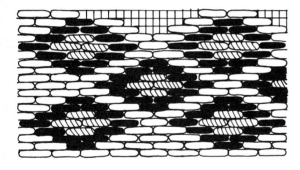

3. Make the centers of the diamond using the second contrasting color yarn, as shown in the same diagram. Fill in around the diamond pattern using the main color yarn.

4. Work in pattern to waist measurement plus 6 inches, tapering 1 end, as shown in *Diagram 8-E2.*

5. Turn margin of tapered end, cutting across tip and folding neatly. Press. Remove masking tape; trim the canvas to within ½ inch of the stitchery.

6. Fold the 2 long ½-inch margins to the wrong side of the belt and press, using a steam iron and a damp cloth.

DIAGRAM 8-E2

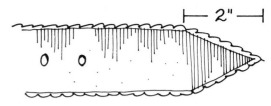

TAPERED END WILL BE COVERED WITH GROSGRAIN

7. Place grosgrain ribbon over wrong side of belt to cover raw canvas margins. Cut ribbon to fit the tapered end of the belt. Spread glue over grosgrain ribbon, leaving unglued 1 inch at straight end and 2 inches at tapered end. Glue in place. Press belt under heavy books. Let dry completely before attaching buckle.

8. Protect belt with waxed paper or aluminum foil. Loop straight end of belt over buckle, leaving ¼ inch of stitchery and ½ inch of raw canvas margin on wrong side. Glue to secure. Trim ribbon to fit if necessary. Turn under raw edge of ribbon and glue to cover raw canvas margin. Let dry completely.

9. Make holes for buckle prong with the pointed end of closed manicure scissors. Make 2 or 3 tiny holes about 1 inch apart, starting 1½ inches from tip of belt. Apply white resin glue lightly around the raw edges of each hole and on both the stitchery and the ribbon sides. Let dry completely.

Sporty Bargello Watchband

DIAGRAM 8-FF

Here's a sporty bargello watchband that's suitable for both sexes and all ages. Although you can purchase watch strap buckles at a jewelry supply store, why not convert an old watchband instead? Remove and clean the old buckle and use the worn band itself to determine the correct dimensions. If you wish to make a wider watchband, see the variation at the end of these directions.

MATERIALS

masking tape
2 pieces canvas mesh, each piece 2 by 8 inches, size #12
2 skeins embroidery floss, in each of 2 contrasting colors
1 tapestry needle
½ yard grosgrain ribbon, ½ inch wide, in color of 1 of embroidery floss skeins
white resin glue
watchband buckle (new or used)

1. Tape edges of canvas to prevent raveling.
2. Work with double strands of embroidery floss. Follow *Diagram 8-F1* for pattern, working vertically over 2 squares of the canvas.

DIAGRAM 8-F1

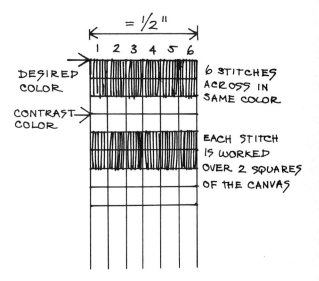

3. Work alternate rows of each color floss on the first piece of canvas until the desired length is reached for the shorter part of the watchband (the part that fits over the buckle). Repeat on the second piece of canvas for the other part of watchband, making it about 2 inches longer. (Determine length of both pieces by measuring length of the old watchband that you are discarding.) Weave in all ends.
4. Trim away excess canvas to within ¼ inch of the stitchery. Fold all ¼-inch margins to the wrong side of the work and press, using a steam iron and a damp cloth. Tuck in corners neatly. Make the work as flat as possible.
5. Cut 2 pieces of grosgrain ribbon to fit the 2 parts of the band. Spread glue on ribbon, leaving unglued ½ inch at both ends of each piece. Position ribbon on wrong sides of work to cover raw canvas margins, and glue in place. Protect with waxed paper or aluminum foil and press flat under heavy books; let dry.
6. Attach 1 band at each side of the watch

by slipping stitchery part through the sprockets (the little metal pieces on each side of a sport watch that hold the band in place). Fold ¼ inch of stitchery and ¼ inch short raw canvas margin to the back of the band. Trim ends of ribbon to fit, and glue securely in place.

7. Slip buckle over end of the short band, pushing prong through stitchery. Fold ¼ inch of stitchery and ¼ inch of raw canvas margin to wrong side. Glue ribbon to cover. Protect straps with aluminum foil or waxed paper, and weight with books until completely dry.

8. Pierce 2 or 3 holes with the points of closed manicure scissors in the longer band. A few drops of white resin glue around these holes on the stitchery and the ribbon sides of the band will prevent fraying. Let dry completely before wearing.

Variation: Directions given are for a ½-inch-wide band. For a 1-inch band, use twice the amount of embroidery floss, 3-inch-wide canvas, and 1-inch-wide grosgrain ribbon. Make bargello rows twice as long as those shown in the diagram.

Suede-Cloth Eyeglass Case

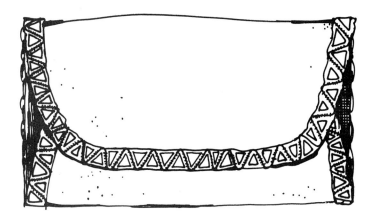

DIAGRAM 8-GG

This rugged suede-look eyeglass case is a handy accessory.

MATERIALS

1 felt rectangle, 9 by 12 inches, in contrasting color to suede cloth

suede cloth, 7 by 10 inches, in any desired color

1 yard gimp upholstery braid, to match suede cloth

5 inches elastic, ½ inch wide, in black

white resin glue

1½ inches nylon fastening tape

1. Cut felt to same size as suede cloth. Round corners of both felt and suede-cloth pieces, as shown in *Diagram 8-G1*.

2. Glue felt to wrong side of suede cloth. Glue gimp braid around the edges of the suede cloth. Protect with waxed paper or aluminum foil, and weight with books until dry.

3. Take the 5-inch strip of elastic. (It will go inside the felt lining to secure the glasses when they are in the case.) Apply glue for 1 inch vertically on the inside (felt side) of the glass case in the center, as shown in *Diagram 8-G2*. Fold elas-

DIAGRAM 8-G1

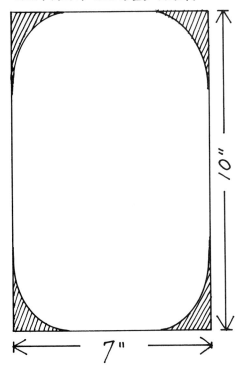

TRIM AWAY SHADED AREA

10"

7"

DIAGRAM 8-G2

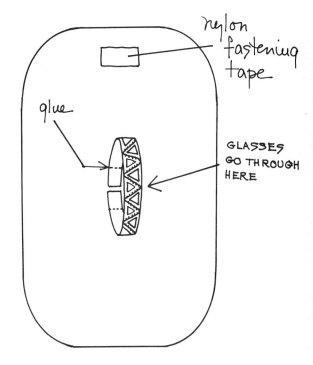

nylon
fastening
tape

glue

GLASSES
GO THROUGH
HERE

tic, and glue both ends in place as shown. Adjust to fit.

4. Glue half the nylon fastening tape to the inside (felt side) of the top flap of the glass case and the other half to the corresponding point on the outside (suede cloth) of the glass case.

Holly-Berry Vest

DIAGRAM 8-HH

Your man will beam with pride when people compliment him (at holiday-time) on his colorful vest. It's made in minutes and is designed to go with the Holly-Berry Bow Tie in the next project.

MATERIALS

brown wrapping paper
¾ yard felt, in red or white
pinking shears (optional)
white resin glue
1⅓ yards fringe, 2½ inches wide, in red, white, or green, or any combination of these colors
1 sheet tracing paper
1 felt rectangle, 9 by 12 inches, or felt scraps, in green
2 balls from ½-inch-diameter ball fringe, in red
1 package no-roll waistband elastic, ¾ inch wide
thread to match large piece of felt
1 hook and eye
3 pieces 1-inch nylon fastening tape or 3 heavy-duty snaps

1. Enlarge vest pattern from *Diagram 8-H1* on brown wrapping paper. Cut out.

2. Cut large felt piece into 4 pieces 18 by 23 inches. Pin pattern to each piece of felt in turn. With pinking shears or regular scissors, cut 4 pattern pieces. (Felt will be doubled to make a fabric with more body.)

3. Match up vest pieces in pairs and glue together around the edges only. Let dry com-

DIAGRAM 8-H1

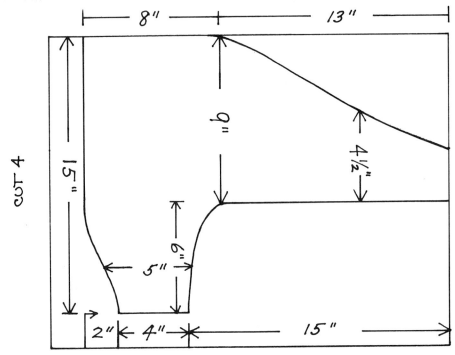

pletely. This makes a doubled left side and a doubled right side.

4. Glue fringe to each side of the front opening from the top of the neckline to the bottom edge of the vest, folding ends of fringe under ¼ inch.

5. Trace holly leaves from *Diagram 8-H2*. Cut out and pin paper pattern to green felt. Repin and cut out pattern for a total of 6 holly leaves, cutting no more than 2 at a time.

6. Glue holly leaves in place on both fronts of the vest, as shown in *Diagram 8-HH*. Glue 1 red ball from ball fringe between leaves where stems meet.

7. On person who will be wearing vest, measure top of 1 shoulder around back of neck to top of other shoulder. Cut elastic to this measurement. With a few stitches, sew elastic to both sides of the neck of the vest on the inside, as in *Diagram 8-HH*.

8. Measure across back waist, and cut another piece of elastic to this measurement. Sew elastic to 1 bottom side of the vest on the inside. Sew a hook on the loose end of this piece of elastic and an eye on the felt at waist to correspond.

9. Lap left front of vest over right so that just the edge of the right fringe shows. Hand-stitch nylon fastening tape or snaps to the outside of the right front of the vest and to the inside of the left front of the vest in corresponding positions.

DIAGRAM 8-H2

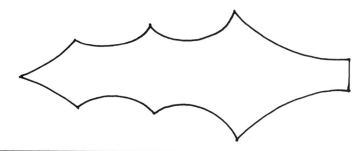

Holly-Berry Bow Tie

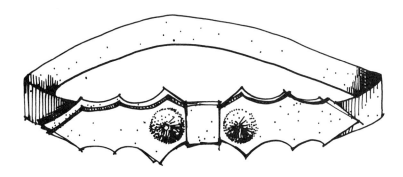

DIAGRAM 8-II

What could be more festive than a holly-berry tie for the man of the house to wear on special holiday occasions? Make your special man this bow tie, to be teamed with the matching vest in the previous project. To make this tie for young boys, simply cut down the pattern to size.

MATERIALS

⅛ yard felt, in green
white resin glue
1 sheet tracing paper
2 balls from ½-inch-diameter ball fringe, in red
1 inch nylon fastening tape

1. Cut a felt strip 2 inches wide and as long as the neck measurement plus 2 inches.

2. Fold the band in half lengthwise; press. Glue to secure. This is the neckband.

3. Trace holly leaves from *Diagram 8-I1;* cut out. Pin pattern on felt and cut 4 pieces of each leaf design.

4. Place 2 sets of leaves together, 1 exactly on top of the other, and glue together at 1 point of leaf. Glue the other set together in the same manner. Let dry.

5. Cut a strip of felt measuring 1 by 2½ inches. Place neckband on table, determine its center, and arrange both sets of leaves around it. Apply glue to 1 small felt strip and place it vertically across center of neckband, making sure the glued leaf points are secured. (See *Diagram 8-I2.*) Overlap ends of short strip on the wrong side of the neckband. Let dry.

6. Glue 1 red ball from the ball fringe to leaves on each side of the center strip and about ¼ inch away, as shown in the sketch.

DIAGRAM 8-I1

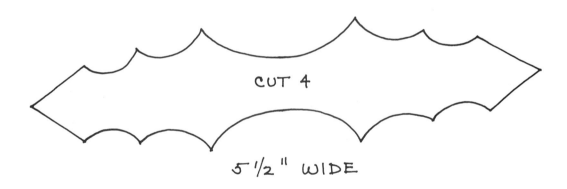

CUT 4

5 ½" WIDE

7. Glue half of nylon fastening tape to the wrong side of 1 end of neckband. Glue other half of nylon fastening tape to the top (right) side of the other end of the neckband. Let dry. (See *Diagram 8-12.*)

8. To wear, fasten neckband with the nylon fastening tape and push under shirt collar so that it is hidden.

DIAGRAM 8-12

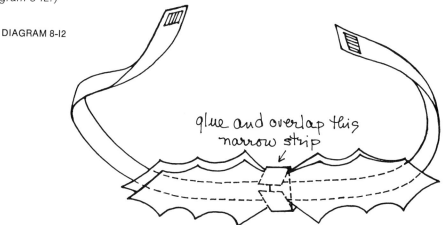

glue and overlap this narrow strip

"Embroidered" Christmas Tie

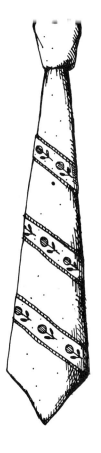

Several years ago I noticed a sedate older gentleman at a holiday cocktail party wearing a cheery red tie decorated with beautiful metallic embroidered ribbon, which I later found out had been bought in Austria. Inspired by my memory of it, I designed this version. I myself wear it with a frilly white blouse and an evening skirt. If you have a number of fancy ribbon scraps lying around, you may want to combine several different ribbons in rows that are closer together than in the directions below. You could even completely cover the tie below the knot with bands of embroidered ribbon in coordinating colors and patterns.

MATERIALS

1 yard embroidered metallic ribbon, ½ inch wide
1 man's silk, synthetic, wool, or cotton necktie, in red or emerald green
white resin glue

1. Starting at the back of the tie 1 or 2 inches from the bottom, pin the ribbon to the tie, tucking the raw end of the ribbon ½ inch under the seam.

2. Bring the ribbon diagonally across the front of the tie and then diagonally across the back, pinning it in place. The ribbon bands on the

tie should be 4 to 5 inches apart. (See *Diagram 8-J1.*)

3. Continue pinning until there is a band of ribbon 16 inches from the bottom of the tie, or until there are 3 bands of ribbon showing on the front. End on the wrong side of the tie, tucking end of ribbon into seam. Do not pin the ribbon much higher than 16 inches or it will interfere with the knot.

4. Glue ribbon carefully to the tie, removing pins as you go. Use glue sparingly. If by chance a spot of glue gets on the tie where it will show, immediately sponge it off with cool water.

5. Press ribboned part of the tie, protected by waxed paper or aluminum foil, under heavy books, and let dry completely.

DIAGRAM 8-J1

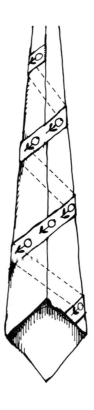